JOB
EVALUATION
In the New World of Work

First published in 2022.

ISBN: 978-1-86922-936-8 (Printed)
eISBN: 978-1-86922-937-5 (PDF eBook)

Published by KR Publishing
Republic of South Africa

Tel: (011) 706-6009
E-mail: orders@knowres.co.za
Website: www.kr.co.za

Typesetting, layout and design: Cia Joubert, cia@knowres.co.za
Cover design: Marlene de'Lorme, marlene@knowres.co.za
Editing and proofreading: Jennifer Renton, jenniferrenton@live.co.za
Project management: Cia Joubert, cia@knowres.co.za

JOB

EVALUATION
In the New World of Work

How to Achieve Equal Pay
for Work of Equal Value

By

Dr Mark Bussin

Dr Christina Swart-Opperman

kr
publishing

2022

ACKNOWLEDGEMENTS

This book would not have been published without the extensive contributions from many very dedicated people.

Thank you to the contributors of the relevant chapters.

Many more of our colleagues, clients and students have inspired us and challenged our thinking – thank you to all.

We applaud the relentless quest for raising the bar of knowledge by all the 21st Century and CO Holdings CC consultants, who continually contribute to innovative discourse and the future way of work.

To Knowledge Resources, thank you for coordinating the production and marketing of this book.

A special thank you to Chris Blair for his insight.

A great thank you to Marina, Daniel, Kate, Genna and James for your inspiration and patience.

My appreciation and thank you to Theo, Armand and Kylie for your support.

Also to all my Namibian clients for allowing me to evaluate jobs galore.

Dr Mark Bussin & Dr C Swart-Opperman
Johannesburg, 2022 + Windhoek, 2022
drbussin@21century.co.za; cso@mweb.com.na
+27 82 901 005; +264 81 129 3088 / +27 81 854 1842

FOREWORD

By Professor Margie Sutherland

In today's fast-paced world, cycle times are getting shorter and shorter. Our organisations are designed like massive military machines, all marching to the beat of one big drum. What is required, however, are pockets of excellence that are quick to respond and can move unhindered and with agility. Organisation design (OD) is a driver of organisational strategy, operational performance, employee commitment, job satisfaction, retention and indeed, Job Evaluation.

The current range of legislative, corporate and organisational reporting demands; the often-critical media reportage and exposés; stakeholder pressure for moral corporate governance; and demands for greater transparency increase the need for this book. Job Evaluation is a difficult skill that needs to be mastered as part of the career capital of human resource managers who are serious about their own futures and credibility. All Executives who serve on, or aspire to serve on, boards of directors and remuneration committees, need a sound body of knowledge of Job Evaluation practices to influence the success of the organisations they serve. This book provides the base for acquiring the knowledge, skills and worldview necessary for accountable leadership.

The insights in this book need to be put to good use and will provide a springboard for career and organisational success. Both authors consistently contribute to the development of a host of business leaders and experts via corporate and consulting experience, wise counsel, writings, and hundreds of lectures, TV and radio interviews. They have upskilled a generation of HR professionals, helped define the field of practice, and made a significant contribution to an international level of excellence in the field.

As a young postgraduate student, Mark was given an article to read on "Super-leadership", in which he learned that to rise to great heights, one has to give away all that one knows to as many people as possible. This he has done tirelessly, informing the worldviews of thousands of individuals and organisations. It is a great pleasure to see the fruits of his career made available to a wide audience in this well-written, usable and value-adding handbook.

Professor Margie Sutherland
Gordon Institute of Business Science, University of Pretoria

TABLE OF CONTENTS

List of Tables

List of Figures

ABOUT THE AUTHORS

Dr Mark Bussin is the Chairperson of 21st Century (Pty) Ltd., a specialist remuneration and Human Resources (HR) consultancy. He has HR and remuneration experience across all industry sectors and is viewed as a thought leader in this arena. Mark has held global executive positions for several multinational organisations, including audit firm, mining, FMCG and financial services organisations. He serves on and advises numerous Boards and Audit and Remuneration Committees. Mark holds a Doctorate in Commerce. He has published or presented over 500 popular articles and papers, and 55 peer-reviewed journal articles. Mark is a guest lecturer at several universities and supervises master's and Doctoral theses in the HR, Leadership and Reward areas. He is a past President of the South African Reward Association (SARA) and a past Commissioner for the remuneration of Public Office Bearers in the Presidency. Mark tutors for WorldatWork globally. Mark enjoys flying Cessnas and loves his family time.

Mark can be contacted at: drbussin@mweb.co.za or on +27 (0)82 901 0055.

Books and Chapters authored by Dr Mark Bussin:

Bussin, M. (2011). *The Remuneration Handbook for Africa*. First edition. Randburg: Knowledge Resources Publishing.

Bluen, S. (2012). T*alent Management in Emerging Markets*. Chapter 6, *Performance management and rewarding talent in emerging markets*. Randburg: Knowledge Resources.

Bussin, M. (2012). T*he Performance Management for Emerging Markets*. Randburg: Knowledge Resources Publishing.

Bussin, M. (2013). *Performance Management for Government, Universities, Schools and NGO's*. Randburg: Knowledge Resources Publishing.

Bussin, M. (2014). *Remuneration and Talent Management*. Randburg: Knowledge Resources Publishing.

Van Eeden, D. (2014). *The Role of the Chief Human Resources Officer*. Chapter 10, *Reward and Recognition*. Randburg: Knowledge Resources Publishing.

Bussin, M. (2015). *Expatriate Compensation*. Randburg: Knowledge Resources Publishing.

Bussin, M. (2012). *The Remuneration Handbook for Africa*. Second edition. Randburg: Knowledge Resources Publishing.

Bussin, M., (2016). *The Remuneration Handbook for Africa*. Third edition. Randburg: Knowledge Resources Publishing.

Bussin, M., & Diez, F. (2017). *The Remuneration Handbook*. International edition. Bryanston: KR Publishing.

Bussin, M., (2017). *Performance Management Reboot*. Bryanston: KR Publishing.

Bussin, M. (2017). *OD for UBER Times*. Bryanston: KR Publishing.

Bussin, M. (2018). *Retention Strategies*. Bryanston: KR Publishing.

Bussin, M. & Blair, C. (2019). *The New World of Work*. Bryanston: KR Publishing.

Bussin, M., (2020). *The Remuneration Handbook for Africa*. Fourth edition. Bryanston: KR Publishing.

Bussin, M., & Diez, F. (2021). *The Remuneration Handbook*. International edition. Second Edition. Bryanston: KR Publishing.

Norman, P. *HR – The New Agenda*. Chapter 7, *Reinventing Remuneration, Benefits and Recognition for the New Now!* Bryanston: KR Publishing.

Dr Christina Swart-Opperman lectures at universities on invitation and supervises master's and Doctoral theses in Organisational Behaviour and People Management areas. Christina has extensive experience in the field of human resources consulting, especially Job Evaluation, and as an industrial psychologist. Christina serves and advises boards in her area of expertise. Christina holds Doctorates in Industrial Psychology (University of Northwest) and Business Administration (University of Cape Town).

Christina can be contacted at: cso@mweb.com.na or +264(0)811 29 3088/ +27 (0)81 865 1842

LIST OF CONTRIBUTORS

Anton Verwey

Barbara Lombard

Belinda O'Regan

Bryden Morton

Chris Blair

Christina Swart-Opperman

Christine Janse Van Rensburg

Daniela Christos

Jaen Beelders

JC Nel

Laurika Fourie

Mark Bussin

Mike Honnet

Morag Phillips

Morris Lamani

Ntombizone (Zone) Feni

OVERVIEW AND CONTEXT

The idea to write this book came from a discussion held between Mark and Christina, who have been heavily involved with Job Evaluation for over 20 years. It was agreed that there was no definitive source to rely on for the numerous mediations, arbitrations and court cases that involve Job Evaluation. The idea of writing a book based on all this experience has finally come to fruition.

The book is presented in such a manner that Job Evaluation is viewed as an important part of the employee experience, impacting the entire employee life cycle.

Chapter 1, *Global changes and UBER times ahead*, opens with a discussion on global trends and the fourth industrial revolution, which has created a different and more challenging context for Job Evaluation. The shift to social dynamics are also deliberated upon.

Chapter 2, *The Rise of the Contingent Workforce* expands on the first chapter by paying specific attention to the agile organisation, characteristics of new work arrangements, and how these play out in the workplace. The role of Job Evaluation as enabler is also discussed.

Chapters 3 and 4 dig into the meaning of Job Evaluation, specifically the Paterson Job Evaluation System. Several key aspects are discussed as they relate to business operations, and their link to job descriptions is elaborated upon. The Paterson System is also proposed as a system that links into the human resources value chain.

Chapter 5, *The Impact of Job Evaluation on Salary Structures*, tackles the crucial aspect of remuneration. Useful guidance on pay structure design is presented, including checklists and tips. The aim is a robust salary structure that is organisational fit.

Chapter 6, *Equal Pay for Work of Equal Value* further describes the different lenses to this concept, and is linked to the emergence thereof during the employee life cycle.

Chapter 7, *Measuring Income Inequality - A Holistic Approach*, identifies multiple methods for identifying and addressing income equality. This chapter presents the ultimate considerations for practitioners: how could income inequalities be addressed in a transparent, responsible manner?

Chapter 8, *Job Evaluation in the New World of Work*, superimposes the idea that no system application is ever perfect. Technology impacts Job Evaluation and this chapter describes the options available. Chapter 9, "The Psychological Impact of the New Way of Job Evaluation" sets out human implications of the new world of work.

* * * *

The new world of work has created unprecedented challenges for human resource practitioners. This book should prompt exciting conversations on the question: What is the role of Job Evaluation?

CHAPTER 1

Global changes and turbulent times ahead

1.1 INTRODUCTION

From an organisation design perspective, we are of the view that two interdependent trends may be worth exploring. These are that: 1) regardless of where you are in the world, the internationalisation of your business is one of the realities you have to deal with; and 2) there is a clear indication (and not a new one) that economic growth and job creation is a function of the well-being of smaller enterprises.

In light of the above, this chapter focuses on global trends, specifically from the perspective of internationalisation. It also highlights some potential implications for organisation design, specifically the creation of agile capability and the knock-on effect on Job Evaluation. We start by discussing the Fourth Industrial Revolution so that we can examine the trends that accompany it.

1.1.1 *The Fourth Industrial Revolution*

The 2016 Davos agenda, confirmed by the *2017 Davos Report*[1], reflected the world's focus on managing successive waves of economic crises by addressing issues such as the stabilisation of the financial system; countering concerns of regional disintegration; and ongoing unemployment, unfulfilled social contracts and inequality in the global economy.

As in previous years, all of these global issues were viewed within the context of a landscape in which emerging technologies play a key role in solving problems of the global commons, from climate change to the future of the Internet, through to new models of public-private co-operation and the application of breakthrough science and technology solutions.[2]

For this reason, much of the debate focused on what is referred to as the Fourth Industrial Revolution (4IR) – the digital revolution that is characterised by a fusion where humans, machines, computers, products and raw materials communicate and cooperate with each other. The 4IR is rapidly blurring the lines between the physical and digital worlds. It is reshaping the economic, social, ecological and cultural contexts in which we live, and requires us to address a rapidly changing global security and humanitarian landscape.[3]

Despite the rapid pace of change and the uncertainties facing the global world, certain trends are inevitable. The section below identifies some of the key macro level global trends. For the purpose of this chapter, a global trend is defined as a longer-term pattern that is currently taking place that could contribute to amplifying global risks and/or alter the relationship between them.

1.2 SOME GLOBAL TRENDS

The following sections name and elaborate on the global trends emerging from the Fourth Industrial Revolution, before a discussion ensues on the global risks. These trends emerge from past occurrences that are expected to repeat themselves, or predictions of things that have not yet happened, but based on expert opinion, will.

1.2.1 *Cyber insecurity*

Growing cyber security issues will challenge governments and businesses, while simultaneously empowering and dislocating individual citizens. It is expected that cyber espionage and attacks by state actors will continue, with attribution remaining difficult. The tug-of-war over privacy versus surveillance and security will also continue, as citizens persist in distrusting their governments on this issue. The world's regulators (such as those in the Netherlands, Canada and Australia) are still scrambling to put into place mandatory data-breach notifications.[4]

1.2.2 *The changing nature of power relationships*

Power is increasingly diffused and fleeting. Leadership voids complicate the ability to develop effective responses to mounting policy challenges. Bremmer suggested that feeble political leaders will increasingly face determined opposition and formidable obstacles as they try to enact their political agendas in their regions.[5] In 2016, the "offense-defence" balance was projected to continue favouring aggressors and abusers of traditional sources of power (for example, cyber attackers), and individuals would be further elated and terrified by the changes underway, from technology to violent extremism. In addition, Bremmer noted that political power play was greater at that time than at any other point since the end of the Cold War.[6]

1.2.3 Global economy

Data from the IMF indicates that in the years leading up to the Covid-19 pandemic, global economic growth was at moderate levels, recording growth of 3.6% and 2.8% in 2018 and 2019 respectively, before plummeting to -3.1% in 2020. At an aggregate level, the global economic response in 2021 was positive, recording growth of 5.9% in 2021, which was expected to remain positive into 2022 and 2023 (4.9% and 3.6% respectively). The global economic growth indicators at an aggregate level are not an indication of how all countries have responded to the economic crisis caused by the Covid-19 pandemic, however. One example is that in Q3 2021, South Africa had fewer employed people than in Q1 2008 as a result of approximately two million jobs being lost since the instatement of the first lockdown in the country in response to the Covid-19 pandemic. Although the aggregate global economic outlook expects a positive outlook and recovery, how evenly this is distributed across the world will determine what it means to any individual country.

1.2.4 Emergence of a global middle class

Growth in emerging regions like Africa and the Middle East will help catalyse the rapidly growing first ever global middle class. This will cause the market for accessible luxury products and services to explode as a result, while the opportunity for global entrepreneurship is democratised. In 2011, rapid growth in consumer markets in the major emerging economies rose from 36% of the total population in to just below 40% in 2015.[7] Among developing economies, the share of the middle class is expected to continue to increase, but more slowly than in recent years. This may give rise to renewed risks of social unrest associated with slower growth in emerging and developing economies.

In these countries, slower growth and unsatisfactory access to middle class living standards may fuel social discontent.[8] These trends may have slowed with the pandemic, but the less than expected impact of Covid-19 on Africa allows some certainty for when the economic recovery starts.

1.2.5 *The continued growth of the collaborative economy*

The sharing economy will continue to explode and will move to profiting the many, not the few. The pandemic, if anything, has heightened this trend. There will be a continued push towards sharing business ecosystems that embrace the "we" instead of the "me" mind-set, to provide value and benefit to the communities they operate in.[9] The notion of businesses, the consumers they serve, and local people seeking freelance employment (and enjoying the benefits thereof) will become more evident and indicative of the permanence of new sharing economies. As Morgan[10] suggested, peer-to-peer sharing in a stagnant wage market is moving from an income boost to a disruptive economic force, which increases value for business, individuals and the community. However, according to the *2022 World Economic Forum Global Risk Report*[11], 40% of the world's people still do not have access to the Internet and may not be able to gain from technology-driven growth.

1.2.6 *Increasing income disparity*

The Organisation for Economic Cooperation and Development (OECD) has indicated that the gap between the rich and poor keeps widening, with the richest 10% of its 34 member states earning 9.5 times the income of the poorest 10%.[12] One of the reasons for the widening wage gap put forward is the growth in non-standard work, which, since the mid-1990s, has included temporary contracts and self-employment. Another reason for the widening wage gap, as cited by Reuben[13], is that global tax and benefit systems have become less effective at redistributing income. According to the International Labour Organisation (ILO)[14], the improvement in the labour market situation in developed economies is limited and uneven. Additionally, in some countries, according to various measures, the middle class has been shrinking. Income inequality, as measured by the Gini index, has risen significantly in most advanced G20 countries. Since the start of the global crisis, top incomes have continued to increase while the poorest 40% of households have fallen behind.[15]

1.2.7 Values will drive new generations

The influence of the "Millennial mind-set" will increase expectations for transparency amongst stakeholders, and declining levels of trust in social institutions will lead to increased demands for the ethical treatment of people. More transparent engagement with society from both business and governments will also be increasingly in demand. Kaiser[16] noted that Millennials are the least racist, least sexist and the least homophobic and xenophobic generation. They are also the most inclusive and collaborative generation. Given that by 2025 Millennials will comprise 75% of the global workforce, Uzialko[17] suggested that the next significant social trend will be incorporating deep social change across all levels of society. This will entail going beyond a philanthropic mindset that (through the provision of products and services) turns hunger and poverty into sufficiency, war into peace, and catastrophic climate change into planetary balance. Failure to embed social change at all levels of society will result in increased stakeholder activism.

Having considered the global trends, the global risks will now be discussed. With awareness of these risks, we are more able to focus our attention on preventing, or combatting, them.

1.3 SOME GLOBAL RISKS

According to the World Economic Forum[18], there are several global risks that remain serious, which because of their combined impact and likelihood, involve some economic risks. Below is a list of the 10 most severe risks on a global scale according to the *World Economic Forum Global Risks Perceptions Report[19]*:

1) Climate action failure (environmental)

2) Extreme weather (environmental)

3) Biodiversity loss (environmental)

4) Social cohesion erosion (societal)

5) Livelihood crisis (societal)

6) Infectious disease (societal)

7) Human environmental damage (environmental)

8) Natural resource crisis (environmental)

9) Debt crises (financial)

10) Geo-economic confrontation (geopolitical)

The broad theme from the above 10 risks is that the environment and society at large are the areas that are expected to face the most severe challenges in the coming years. This should stress the urgency for business to adopt strategies that pursue the fulfilment of ESG (economic, social, governance) goals, as two of these areas are include the eight most severe risks on a global scale. As a stakeholder of the global economy, business can strive to effect change in these ESG areas, which would have a positive impact on alleviating some of these risks.

1.4 PRACTICAL CONSIDERATIONS

As is so often the case with perspectives of this nature, the question arises "So what?" After all, these trends (and we highlighted only a few) are for the most part beyond the control or even influence of individual leaders or businesses. How do we prevent this from becoming just another interesting philosophical conversation? In essence, what role can you play to mitigate the risks arising from the global trends emerging from the Fourth Industrial Revolution?

At a practical level, there are a series of possibilities that you could consider. One suggestion is that you engage your management team on a "fact-based" exploration of the environment you have to compete in. Consider the stakeholders who are involved in this environment. These stakeholders are who you will be affecting and who will be affecting you. Play out the scenario in your head of how each interaction will ensue and what the consequences are for each. Consider implementing processes to change the mind-set with which the different levels of your leadership teams think about and engages with the business. Rethink the type of organisation capacity you will need to not only compete, but thrive in such a challenging environment. Build the talent you need, not only for now, but also for the future. Be focused on understanding customer and stakeholder expectations and how you could make them central to your business purpose.

1.5 ORGANISATION DESIGN APPLICATION

The current global pandemic is a socio-economic crisis and a very emotional event that caught most businesses, globally and locally, unaware in terms of moving rapidly from a traditional corporate structure to a mostly remote workforce arrangement, at best. At worst, companies are having to consider their sustainability, making difficult and business-changing decisions in an unpredictable and fast-moving environment. It has become clear that the impact from the pandemic will not be short term, but will affect countries for years to come, changing economic development and social cohesion[20]; there is no aspect of life that will not be impacted in one form or another. For companies, this constant state of uncertainty and crisis management places pressure on their organisational systems, impacting decisions from business strategy to people management. There is a need to balance the pressure from shareholders and those of employees; in a pandemic, which pressure takes precedence? What options exist for companies to manage the pandemic with an eye on longevity and survival? And what opportunities exist in a 'forced change' workplace environment that may change the way companies operate from now on?

Our view is that the new world of work will be a blended approach – some online, some in person, some at home and some at your place of choice. This is the 'new normal' that companies must navigate, embracing agility and innovation, adapting strategy, and managing people to ensure resilience and commitment during very uncertain times. It will impact Job Evaluation and pay scale design and principles in a way not experienced before.

1.5.1 *Managing (people) costs*

One of the most common factors businesses must consider under stress is cost reduction. This may result in retrenchments, furloughing employees, or cutting salaries and wages (with or without an associated reduction in working hours).

Maréchal, Sebastian and Puppe investigated whether wage cuts damage morale.[21] As the authors argue, staff morale is imperative for workers to remain committed and directed towards achieving the company's goals. Wages are seen as a reflection of the morale and level of commitment, which is especially important when wages are not linked to specific outputs (for instance a target of x products sewn). The authors found that while wage reductions impacted morale and productivity, wage increases had no significant impact on productivity. But would this be the case when the trade-off for employees is retrenchment? And do the co-occurring national feelings of social cohesion, staying at work and assisting society with altruism during a pandemic impact the results?

An alternative to wage cuts (which are a cut in financial remuneration without the associated cut in time) is work sharing arrangements. Work sharing is more likely to be used during a crisis such as a pandemic, when the sustainability of the company is financially at risk but continuing productivity is essential. Work sharing includes the reduction of work hours instead of retrenchment. In this way, all workers remain employed, versus a smaller number being laid-off. Shelton argues that work sharing arrangements may help with employee morale.[22] The compounding impact of isolation, reduced working hours and perceived loyalty to a company during the pandemic would be interesting to ascertain. Kiviat[23] argued that work sharing is preferential to retrenchments as staff who remain employed may have "survivor's guilt", impacting morale with emotional contagion and lowering productivity. It may well be the case that the impact of retrenchments on staff who remain would impact productivity and a cost-benefit analysis would need to be considered. As Shelton pointed out, "For employers, the decision between layoffs and an arrangement combining work sharing with Short Time Compensation (STC) may rest on both financial and non-quantifiable factors such as employee morale. Some firms may find that the combination of work sharing and STC helps reduce total costs during a downturn; however, other firms may find that layoffs are more cost-effective".[24]

Time and wages are not the only consideration in managing people costs appropriately while ensuring employee morale and loyalty. In a pandemic, it may be the case that employees are more loyal to companies they trust or whose values they align with.[25] For instance, Isenhour[26] argued that companies should consider that employees may trade-off job prestige over pay, aligning with their cultural values. The response and adaptation to the pandemic have highlighted and forced new ways of working, some of which have been proposed for some time.[27]

1.6 CONCLUSION

For some years now, we have held the view that a fundamental trend affecting business at the global, regional and national levels is a shift in social dynamics. This sense of social disruption is not new; in 1998, Nicoll wrote in Parker that, "Humanity finds itself mid-stride between an old and new era and we have not yet found our way. We know the old no longer works, yet the new is not yet formed clearly enough to be believed. We are developing a new story and in the process of altering much of what we think, feel and do."[28]

The Covid-19 pandemic is sure to change the way we work.[29] At the very least, companies are assessing their preparedness for a 'black swan' event, the impact on business continuity, and how employees and customers have responded. Virtual meetings, online collaboration and agile ways of working are becoming normal in workplaces that can use these strategies. Organisations are finding new ways to remain connected to their customer base, ensuring their communication is transparent and unambiguous.

The socio-economic impact of the pandemic will last for some time, with shrinking global growth and constrained global trade, but also new areas of innovation and opportunities for fast recovery as the pandemic resolves.[30] As companies use this time to innovate, change their ways of working, adapt and respond to the impact of the pandemic, so resilience is built.

The next chapter, Chapter 2, discusses the contingent workforce and the new world of work. It highlights the curve-ball that has been thrown at our current systems, for instance the Job Evaluation system, which will have to be adapted to accommodate a new type of workforce.

CHAPTER 2

The Rise of the Contingent Workforce

2.1 INTRODUCTION

The ever changing economic, environmental, social and political landscapes are constantly challenging organisations to adapt and respond. A focus on the agility of organisations is highlighted by the growth in the start-up and accelerator models that are prevalent globally. Organisations as we know them, although often promoting the need for agility, are most times still structured in a manner that suits post-industrial revolution foundations and concepts. The mind-set of how we structure organisations is slow moving and impacted or limited by counteractive factors such as labour laws impacting the move to individuals being 'contingents' with very few employee protections. The argument, however, may be that we are not seeing the rise of the contingent workforce, which has already begun, but rather the adoption and entrenchment thereof. The world of work is ever changing, with one of the most apparent and obvious trends being that of a more fluid and flexible workforce.

As Crous noted, agile methodologies are transforming management and organisations.[31] These methodologies are underpinned by a new set of values, principles, practices and processes. This is a significant shift from the traditional command-and-control style management, which is unable to keep pace with change or new economic conditions. Old methods are one of the main reasons organisations are finding themselves unable to compete, however the contingent workforce allows an organisation to expand and contract during times of opportunities and downturns. We will begin by considering a definition and explanation of the contingent workforce, before discussing what changes ensue with the growth of this type of workforce.

2.2 THE CONTINGENT WORKFORCE

When we think of the word 'contingent', the first thought that comes to mind is that of an alternative or a back-up plan for an unexpected, yet possibly anticipated, event. This is the exact concept and driver behind the rise of the contingent workforce, good examples of which are Fiverr, Freelancer and Upwork.[32, 33, 34] In the case of unexpected business requirements, opportunities or issues, organisations often turn to their alternative providers, who are not employees but may support them during times of increased work and specialised projects. In the changing world of work and the manner in which businesses operate these days, in order to provide a differentiated service and scale where the need arises, they have to consider the need for agility. Traditional hiring practices and large workforces may impact an organisation's capability to scale to unexpected client demands and then downscale when the demand subsides. This is one of the reasons why organisations are increasingly relying on a contingent workforce in their planning and operating models.[35] It is expected that in the world post-Covid-19, the contingent workforce is likely to increase.

For the individual contributor, the 'employee', the shift from having a job for life to shorter job stints or freelance work may have arisen from the uncertainty the economy has left them in. The ideal of having one job or one career for life may also no longer be in line with the values and motives of why and where people choose to work. This makes the employee a contingent employee. A contingent workforce, therefore, is a labour pool where people are hired as and when needed. Usually this workforce consists of consultants, freelancers, independent contractors and any other person not on the company payroll. They can operate in the organisation or remotely, but do have fewer benefits and less pay than full-time workers.[36] In South Africa, the Labour Relations Act provides some protection to contingent and temporary workers, but under specific conditions. If a person works more than three months on a full-time basis, they are, in fact, considered permanent employees.[37]

The table below illustrates the differences between a 'standard' and a 'contingent' workforce.

Table 2.1: Differences between a traditional workforce and a contingent workforce

Traditional/Standard Arrangement	Contingent/Non-Standard Arrangement
Defined long term contract	Contracts are generally short term and less defined or robust. Generally "zero" hour contracts, but the understanding is there that should a requirement arise, they will be contracted.
Anticipated continuous relationship	Relationship is project-based; it may continue but is not guaranteed or expected.
Defined job requirements that are usually limited to one function/role	May have a number of differing 'job titles' depending on offering.
Set and capped remuneration	Remuneration is based on projects and negotiated.
Set hours (although companies expect more than set hours)	Hours are set but more project-based; some contingent workers have zero hour contracts but are on call for defined projects.
Benefits and rewards	No benefits offered by the company generally, but contingent employees find benefits of flexibility, variety of work, uncapped remuneration etc.
Working space and resources such as a PC provided by the company	Has own infrastructure in most cases.
A manager	A client
A team	A project team; independent workers
Expectation of the company promoting their brand and careers (employer-driven)	Promotion of own brand and career (person-driven)
Paid via traditional payrolls	May submit invoices for work done and manage own tax payments

Concerning the above, how did these differences arise? Section 2.3. provides some insight into this question.

2.3 THE EVOLUTION OF THE CONTINGENT WORKFORCE

The rise of the contingent workforce is likely to have been driven as much by participants in the workforce as by the agility requirements of businesses. Millennials (individuals who reached young adulthood in the early years of the 21st century) are expecting a different working experience to what their parents and grandparents accepted. Not only do they require a differing environment, however, but they are often unlikely to associate themselves with one brand, especially if that brand is not congruent with their values and principles.

A key driver of the contingent model is that of flexibility not only for the employer, but for "the contingents" themselves. Contingent employees are interested in flexibility not only of the working environment and set-up, but also of the work they are exposed to and involved in. The contingent model appears to have benefits for both parties, with the employer being able to react to large scale projects and opportunities without having the burden of a defined and expensive organisational structure. In a study by OCG it was found that:

> "One of the biggest impacts of the contingent workforce is the creation of flexibility for both employee and employer. For employees, working on a temporary or contract basis ensures that they have full control of their career, and allows them to do a wide variety of work, often for a range of clients. For employers, having a flexible workforce means that an organisation can easily scale their labour capability to the level they require. If there is a high demand for work, they can easily add more people with the necessary skills. On the other hand, if they are experiencing a work shortage, they are able to easily reduce costs as contingent workers are not as difficult to release as permanent ones. The access to this large contingent talent pool makes the management of large projects far easier, and less costly. Our survey indicated that this was the main reason for engaging contingent staff, with 17.8% of respondents indicating that this was the main benefit of contingent workers to their company".[38]

As the contingent workforce increases, so the need for job grading becomes necessary. Employers thus need to plan appropriately, as the contingent employee is able to use job grading as a means to evaluate positions. This adds a level of protection for both employers and employees. A study conducted by the independent research firm Edelman Intelligence, which was commissioned in partnership with Upwork and Freelancers Union, predicted in 2017 that by 2027 the majority of the US workforce would be contingent. It is likely that post the Covid-19 pandemic, contingent jobs may not just be a preferred trend but a necessity in the economic recovery.

PeopleTicker provides a concise and informative overview of the drivers and evolution of the rise of the contingent workforce, which is illustrated in Figure 2.1 below:

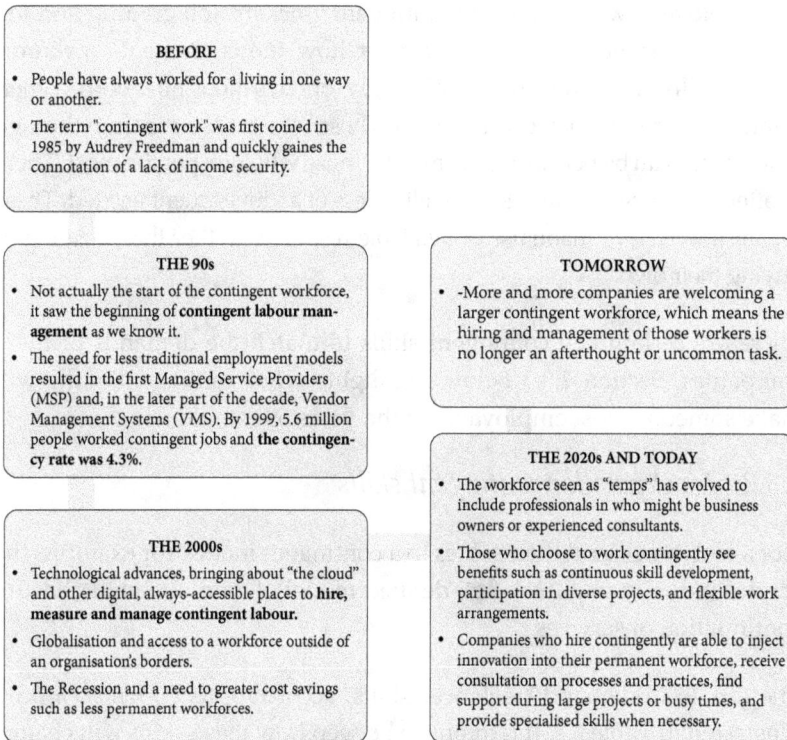

BEFORE
- People have always worked for a living in one way or another.
- The term "contingent work" was first coined in 1985 by Audrey Freedman and quickly gaines the connotation of a lack of income security.

THE 90s
- Not actually the start of the contingent workforce, it saw the beginning of **contingent labour management** as we know it.
- The need for less traditional employment models resulted in the first Managed Service Providers (MSP) and, in the later part of the decade, Vendor Management Systems (VMS). By 1999, 5.6 million people worked contingent jobs and **the contingency rate was 4.3%**.

THE 2000s
- Technological advances, bringing about "the cloud" and other digital, always-accessible places to **hire, measure and manage contingent labour.**
- Globalisation and access to a workforce outside of an organisation's borders.
- The Recession and a need to greater cost savings such as less permanent workforces.

TOMORROW
- -More and more companies are welcoming a larger contingent workforce, which means the hiring and management of those workers is no longer an afterthought or uncommon task.

THE 2020s AND TODAY
- The workforce seen as "temps" has evolved to include professionals in who might be business owners or experienced consultants.
- Those who choose to work contingently see benefits such as continuous skill development, participation in diverse projects, and flexible work arrangements.
- Companies who hire contingently are able to inject innovation into their permanent workforce, receive consultation on processes and practices, find support during large projects or busy times, and provide specialised skills when necessary.

Figure 2.1: Overview of the drivers and evolution of the rise of the contingent workforce (adapted from PeopleTicker[39])

The contingent workforce had certain influencers in its existence – otherwise considered disrupters. The section below analyses these disrupters for further insight into the causality of the contingent workforce that defines our way of work today.

2.3.1   *The disrupters in the world of the contingent workforce*

A key disrupter of the traditional sourcing and talent acquisition models are online employment platforms. These take several forms – from the providers of platforms where employers can search for talent and often hire in a more traditional way, to true online platforms that assist organisations in the resourcing of their contingent models. These platforms may be seen as the "Uber" of the world of employment. They offer a massive workforce for use on demand without actually employing such individuals, but rather provide the platform to match up 'employers' with transient/contingent workers. Job grading and Job Evaluation are necessary as a base for how the contingent workforce will be utilised by employers. Seemingly, organisations now borrow their commodities rather than owning them. Those who act as a medium through which work can be performed seem to be those who prosper the most. There is, after all, less risk in process, as well as less of an investment needed. These organisations have made use of available resources, rather than creating or buying their own.[40]

There are certain key contingent skills to match the demands of these companies. Section 2.3.3 below highlights what contingent skills will make someone most employable in the years to come.

2.3.2   *Most popular contingent skills*

Not all job types lend themselves to a contingent model, for example, the service industry requires a set, defined model of employment to ensure continuation of services.

The top 25 in demand freelancer skills, according to *Entrepreneur*, are illustrated in Table 2.2. It remains to be seen how these skills will change and expand post the pandemic.

Table 2.2: Top 25 in demand freelancer skills (Source: Rampton)[41]

1. Natural language processing	9. Brand strategy	18. Bluetooth specialist
2. Swift development	10. Business consulting	19. Stripe specialist
3. Social media management	11. Machine learning	20. SEO/Content writing
4. Amazon Marketplace Web Services (MWS)	12. 3D rendering	21. Virtual assistant
5. AngularJS development	13. Zendesk customer support	22. Immigration law
6. MySQL programming	14. Information security	23. Accounting (CPA)
7. Instagram marketing	15. R development	24. Photography/video editing
8. Twilio API development	16. User experience design	25. Voiceover artists
	17. Node.js development	

Considering there is a new way of work – contingent work – the next assumption to be made is that the psychological contract has been altered to accommodate this type of workforce. Below we consider this assumption to answer whether this is the case or not.

2.4 DOES A CONTINGENT WORKFORCE NEED A NEW PSYCHOLOGICAL CONTRACT?

In traditional employment relationships there is what is termed a 'psychological contract'. This contract is defined in the *Penguin Dictionary of Psychology* as "the unwritten set of expectations that exists between the persons in a relationship, the members of a group, the people who work for an organisation etc. The term is used most often in industrial/ organisational psychology, where it includes the levels of performance that each member of an organisation is expected to reach and each member's own expectations with respect to salary, advancement, benefits, prerequisites etc. Moreover, such nebulous components like the quality of life, job satisfaction, personal fulfilment and the like are implicitly part of the contract".[42]

In the contingent world, the psychological contract is turned on its head. Individuals are now accountable for diversification of opportunities in order to support their own expectations and growth needs. The employer is no longer tacitly responsible for these, although they possibly expect an even higher level of performance as they are not bound to retain services or engage on projects again should performance not be up to par. The concept of an employee lacking motivation to compete their work and being provided with support and mentorship from the organisation is not relevant in the model of contingent work. With this concept in mind, the thought may be that the contingent employee could feel isolated and disengaged as they have no support, or sense of belonging. The question is, however, do they want to 'belong'? Where do they find the motivators and drivers for engagement? Are they engaged with the organisation or the work?

The answer may come from people's need for freedom. Even though they may be foregoing the "security" of a predictable pay check, they are gaining the freedom to work in different fields and on new projects, and can define their own models of work. The new psychological contract may possibly be defined as "a relationship that is transient in nature whereby individuals come together for the successful completion of a specific task/project and then part ways with no commitment to each other. Each participant has defined what they need to get out of the relationship from an expectation perspective relating to financial rewards which are completely defined and not movable unless the scope changes or rewards are not financial in nature but altruistic, personally satisfying or challenging. The intangible elements of the relationship to ensure performance is the possible consequences of being poorly rated on work platforms where these relationship matches are made and hence the possible impact on not acquiring future transient projects and a tarnish on one's own personal branding. Engagement is with the work or project and not the organisation".[43]

Having discussed the process of including contingent workers in your workforce, the next section addresses the contingent culture and whether contingent workers should be included in the company culture or not.

2.4.1 *The contingent culture*

A question often considered when hiring a contingent workforce is whether they should be engaged with the company culture or not. As the contingent worker is likely to work for more than one employer, is it possible for them to still feel engaged with the values and culture of the 'client' they are working for? In an OCG study it was found that 86% of employers feel they are giving contingent workers the same treatment as permanent employees, however 19% of contingent workers feel they are not engaged with a company culture. This shows that employers are perhaps not doing enough to make contingent workers feel at home in the company, and should involve them more in company culture outside of just working. Despite this, the long-held perception that contractors have a negative impact on company culture seems to be a little wide of the mark. Only 4.6% of employers feel this is the case, and 92.5% of employees believe that contingent work is becoming more accepted. This bodes well for further growth of the contingent workforce in the future, as contingent workers become more accepted by both employees and employers alike, completely dispelling the idea that they have a negative effect on company culture.[44]

Incorporating contingent workers into the culture is a mechanism whereby the relationship continues beyond "the gig". By incorporating contingent workers into the culture, employers build relationships and enjoy the benefits of having a pool of talented, competent people who understand the values of the business. We now also need to adapt HR practices to accommodate these individuals. The means by which we can do so are discussed next.

2.5 ADAPTING HR PRACTICES TO ACCOMMODATE THE CONTINGENT WORKFORCE

The traditional HR processes and policies are not necessarily applicable to the new workforce. Most organisations are also not necessarily effectively planning their contingent workforce requirements, and hence not building models to accommodate new workers and create a flexible yet less transient relationship. This type of work arrangement has its benefits in that the organisation does not have sunk costs, but they also do not have an ongoing contract with people who have built their capabilities and competencies. A partner at a big consulting firm noted that it is important to create some form of connection with contingent employees, keeping them connected with the organisation so that they may return for further projects.[45]

Dylan White, a Senior Partner at Denovo, advised that HR needs to build in clear policies and processes for managing the workforce, with a mind-shift change regarding the concept of revenue generation with each project, and an even stronger understanding of the business objectives and scope of the project.[46] He added that there is still a need to include the contingent workforce in induction and training processes to instil the company's values and processes.

An additional factor that organisations traditionally have not managed effectively is tracking contingent workers' costs, as well as monitoring productivity. In the OCG study, *The Rise of the Contingent Workforce*, it was found that 75% of employers do not measure how much is being spent on contingent labour and whether it is effectively spent, and 85% of employers do not measure the productivity of contingent workers.[47]

Despite the increased number of contingent workers in the workforce, not all organisations are equipped to have them on board. There are several organisational limitations that prevent the successful use of contingent workers, which are discussed in the next section.

2.6   THE CONTINGENT WORKFORCE – BARRIERS TO ENTRY

Most professional services firms agree that HR professionals may not always be aware of the risks and issues they may expose their organisation to when hiring contingent employees, and not all organisations have defined policies and procedures to mitigate risks when hiring contingent employees.[48]

Although organisations are moving to contingent models, a key barrier to entry often expressed by HR professionals is **in-country labour laws,** which may prevent the procurement of services in this manner. In addition to this, organisations are concerned about privacy legislation, loss of intellectual property, lack of confidentiality and possible brand damage.

The keys to an effective contingent programme are planning, defined approaches and projects. It cannot be as ad hoc and unplanned as initially believed or implemented. In order to anticipate risks and barriers while still attaining the benefits of cost saving, an elastic workforce and access to a pool of skills, an organisation should do the following:

- Define the relationship clearly upfront and have consistent approaches to this definition.

- Have standard and mandatory NDAs that contingent workers are required to sign at the start of each engagement.

- "Know" and research your contingent worker as well as you would a core employee through reference checks, online ratings, CVs, qualification confirmations etc.

- Make use of platforms that provide clear mechanisms for on-boarding a worker onto a project and off-boarding them once the project is complete. The cost is worth it.

- Get line managers to account for the use of contingent workers as clearly as hiring permanent core employees. The management of costs and an analysis of returns should be a requirement.[49]

2.7 CONCLUSION

There is an abundance of literature relating to the benefits, risks and rise of the contingent workforce. The move to this model is rapid in some regions and minimal in others. As organisations and employees find themselves facing the challenges of an uncertain economy, down-sizing and up-sizing, there is a need not only for organisations to embrace the new way of working, but its people as well. The big question is: do these contingent workers need their jobs evaluated? Well, not if they are genuine contract workers, but it may still be useful if you want to get a benchmark idea for what the "contract price" should be – it could approximate the total annual remuneration of your full-time staff.

The next chapter discusses the importance of Job Evaluation, providing insights into its emergence, the need for it in organisations, and the factors required to guarantee its success.

CHAPTER 3

What is Job Evaluation?

3.1 INTRODUCTION

Job evaluation is the **systematic** and **objective** process of comparing one job to another within an organisation to arrive at different job levels or a hierarchy. Job sizing is an outcome of Job Evaluation and is like a ruler or scale – it tells you the "size" or "weight" of the job. The purpose is to size all jobs in an organisation from smallest to biggest using a scale. From an employee justice perspective, the level or size of one's job is important, and adds to personal motivations based on reward and growth. From an employer perspective, job sizes create certainty for planning and resource allocation.

Job evaluations must be objective; they cannot consider individual characteristics, personalities or performance. Individual abilities and efforts may be taken into account and reflected in an employee's earnings, but that is entirely different from the grading of the job; Job Evaluation grades the job, not the person. Neither individual effort nor labour market conditions are taken into account when conducting a grading. Having said this, many remuneration experts consider Job Evaluation (or job sizing) as necessary for remuneration decisions to be made, including pay scale and fringe benefits. For this reason, it needs to be objective, defendable and rigorously executed.

Benefits of Job Evaluation systems include the provision of a logical graded hierarchy and pay structure. In this way, inequalities are reduced, and management and employees are able to see how different jobs relate to one another. Job evaluation provides a way to regain control over salary and wage administration, ensuring a consistent rationale for pay structures. Wage and salary administration are seen to be fair, and a detailed analysis of wage and skills gaps becomes possible. In addition, negotiation and collective bargaining are made easier by using a common language or defined point of reference. Compliance with legislation for those countries that have pay equity legislation is a considerable advantage.

There are a number of Job Evaluation systems in the market (see annexure 1 for some commonly used systems), but they all essentially rank jobs in an organisation from smallest to largest in terms of the **complexity** of the job. It is less important which system is used, than finding the system that works best for the workplace it is being applied in. Overall, consider a system that is defendable. In effect, it must be easy to understand and implement, be well regarded in the field, and very importantly, be endorsed and understood by the Executive and Remuneration Committees.

3.1.1 *Background of Job Evaluation*

Over the years, Job Evaluation has been adjusted to eliminate discrimination on the basis of pay. Today, Job Evaluation continues to represent employees to ensure fairness and is continually improved as society progresses. Thus, having analysed the shaky start of job analysis, the next section highlights its importance and its necessity.

3.2 THE NEED FOR JOB EVALUATION AT ALL STAGES OF A BUSINESS LIFECYCLE

As companies grow from being owner managed, more formal systems need to be implemented that "explain" why employees should earn what they earn. Job evaluation and salary structures provide the cornerstone for this explanation.

When organisations are first formed the owner has some idea of what tasks are performed in every job, what person is required to fill that post, and how much to pay this person. Usually, this "pay policy" can be justified to employees. The employee usually has a one-on-one relationship with the manager and negotiation around the remuneration issue is informal and sometimes frequent.

As the organisation grows it becomes more structured, with more processes and systems necessary for the owner/manager to control. Various sections are created, and sectional managers become responsible for the hiring, firing and remuneration levels of staff. The changing perception of management and the varied priorities between section managers lead to discrepancies in pay rates between divisions, and even between jobs with similar skills. At this stage, Job Evaluations are usually used. Although Job Evaluations help to determine relative pay levels, the pay levels for particular jobs and individual earnings remain organisational policy decisions based on internal and external factors.

Benefits which accrue from job descriptions and the process of writing them provide an opportunity to study the organisational structure and to identify anomalies, since the job analyst has to understand fully how each job is structured. The following must be noted by the job analyst: key areas of responsibility, levels of authority and accountability, reporting relationships, spans of control, lines of communication, job design and resourcing levels. Finally, most countries have legislation around pay equity or equal pay for work of equal value. Having a Job Evaluation system goes a long way to comply with this type of legislation because one can more easily explain why certain categories of employees earn commensurate amounts of pay.

3.2.1 When should Job Evaluation be used?

Job evaluation is a logical follow through in support of organisational design, which in turn is a response to organisation strategy. Many of the problems that inhibit the effectiveness of organisations have to do with job or role perceptions. Sorting out problems of job definition and relativities can often dispose of the root cause. It is often easier to see career paths that facilitate skills development, especially under the job family modelling or career path approach.

Job evaluations should be applied in situations where discrepancies are seen in interdepartmental hierarchies regarding job values. They should also be applied where salaries and wages are not equitably distributed. Job evaluations and salary structures provide useful data for analysing an organisation's pay slope, pay ratios, pay ranges and overlap. There are legislative requirements asking companies for this type of data, thus some kind of Job Evaluation system is needed in order to fulfil submission requirements.

There are various circumstances that require Job Evaluation. One such circumstance is when a range of pay rates exist for variety of reasons.

Job evaluations may also be used when there are demands for parity. Two completely different job roles may require the same skill level, thus Job Evaluation needs to be used to categorise these jobs equally. Alternatively, two job roles may seem similar but have different prerequisites to perform them. Job evaluation will therefore need to be used to categorise them.

Job evaluation should be used to co-ordinate pay rates. When minimal coordination of pay rates exists, this makes the pay system disorganised and unjustified. Additionally, Job Evaluation should be used to bring organisation to the basis of pay rates; it should form a logical basis upon which to make pay decisions. Job evaluation is needed when "job values" are confused with "person values". For instance, person A fills job 1. Job 1 is generally worth $20 an hour but since person 1 has a great personality, the employer decides to give them $40 an hour. Person 1 decides to leave the job and the next employee, person 2, although equally as competent as person 1, has less personality and gets paid $20 an hour. Thus, the pay system has worked on a "person" basis by valuing the employee, rather than valuing the job.

Another purpose of Job Evaluation is for when organisational structure reviews are required. Experts can choose to reorganise the organisational structure with the help of job grades as per the evaluation process. It can also help with the development of career paths.

Ultimately, Job Evaluation should be applied in situations where discrepancies are seen in interdepartmental hierarchies regarding job values. It should also be applied where salaries and wages are not equitably distributed.

There are thus a variety of reasons for Job Evaluations to be undertaken. On the whole, the reasons are usually centred around parity, transparency and planning. To this end, Job Evaluations can be used as a means of facilitating the evolution of the organisation, helping management and employees see how different jobs relate to each other, plotting career paths through the hierarchy, assisting with skills development within the workplace, and conducting a detailed analysis of wage and skills gaps for providing a common language and defined point of reference for negotiation and collective bargaining.

Benefits which will accrue from job descriptions and the process of writing them include detailed information for recruitment, specifically for developing the job specification; planning the interview; meaningful advertising; providing prospective employees with details of what is required in the job; and meaningful induction training. Apart from assisting in the understanding of the organisational structure and informing the recruitment process, there are additional benefits accruing from job descriptions which are discussed in the below section.

Further benefits which accrue from job descriptions and the process of writing them are that they supply a basis for job procedures and performance standards, a framework for performance and progress review, detailed information for career pathing and resource planning, and detailed information for the development of training programmes. They also assist the organisation to comply with legislation that requires organisations to justify differences in pay. Having discussed the benefits of job descriptions, the next section outlines the Job Evaluation process.

Table 3.1: Definition of terms relating to Job Evaluation

Term	Definition
Job analysis	The process of examining the content of a job and breaking it down into its tasks, functions, minor functions, processes, operations and elements.
Job description	The description of a job as a result of job analysis.
Job evaluation	The whole process put together.
Job grading	The ranking or assigning of levels to jobs as a result of job analysis.
Job specification	The qualifications, experience and personal qualities required by the jobholder (mainly used for recruitment).
Wage and salary structures	The assignment of a monetary value to each grade, based on: • affordability; • market norms and rates; • employee representation negotiations; and • economic environment and indicators.

3.3　JOB EVALUATION PROCESS

During the process of Job Evaluation, questions should be asked about the tasks being performed in a particular job, the relationship of jobs to each other, overlapping job content, and responsibilities. The content provided in the job descriptions can be effectively used for job design and job enrichment programmes. Job evaluation systems have to be flexible to accommodate the changing, dynamic environments within the market as well as in the organisation.

There are two stages in Job Evaluations:

- **Stage 1:** Only the job is graded, and only in its current state. This is not an idealistic future job and it needs to be considered as though there are no incumbents. Always consider competence in evaluating the role, not 'what could go wrong'. Job descriptions and a grade result.

- **Stage 2:** After the job has been graded, only then do you look at individuals in the job and decide where to place them on the pay scale. This results in a salary structure.

Job evaluation must be an impersonal process in stage 1; it must not consider the quality, performance or effort that a person brings to the job so as to avoid bias. One must be cautious that the current wage or salary structure in an organisation does not introduce bias. Consciously or unconsciously, we tend to construct a hierarchy of jobs in our own minds based on what we know of the existing wage or salary structure. The grading committee must continually be reminded that it is "the job and not the person" that is important, and that current wage or salary levels are irrelevant to the grading process. It is only in the development of the salary or remuneration structure at stage 2 that one can take personal qualities, the characteristics of the person in the job, performance and effort into account.

In job grading, assessment and comparison focus on the job content, not the value of a job to the organisation. Although Job Evaluation is used to determine relative pay levels, pay levels for particular jobs and individual earnings remain organisational policy decisions based upon internal and external factors. Internal equity and external equity features

28

are used to compile the salary structure. Figure 3.1 below shows a typical salary structure.

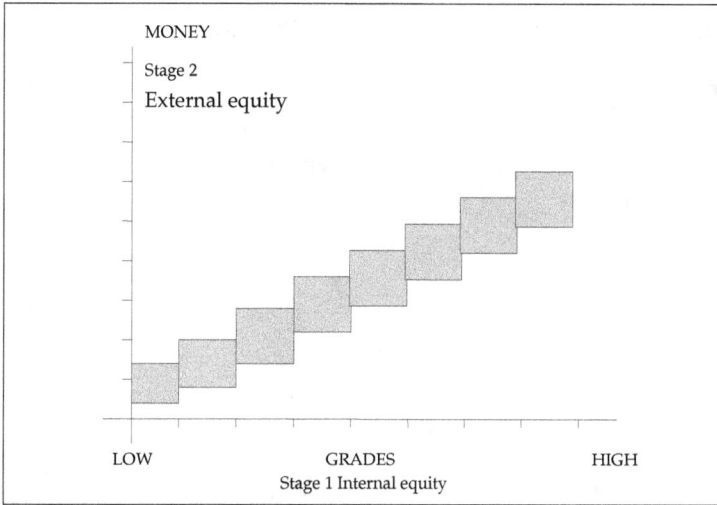

Figure 3.1: Typical salary structure

3.3.1 *Job descriptions and job grading (stage 1)*

The processes of developing job descriptions and conducting job grading are set out in the below.

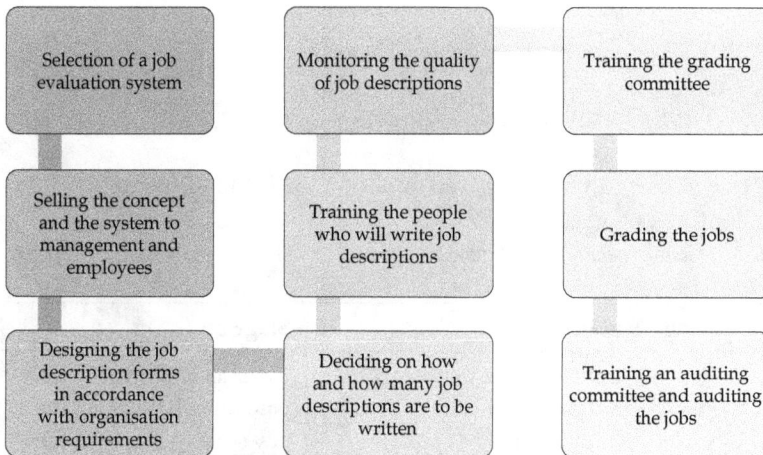

Figure 3.2: Job descriptions and job grading: Stage 1

This process is inflexible; one must observe the grading rules if the system is to retain its credibility. To enable the grading committee to grade jobs objectively, job descriptions must be written. Most systems of Job Evaluation require job descriptions if gradings are to be justified.

3.3.2 Salary structure (stage 2)

Stage 2 is a separate process, with seven steps which are outlined in Figure 3.3 below.

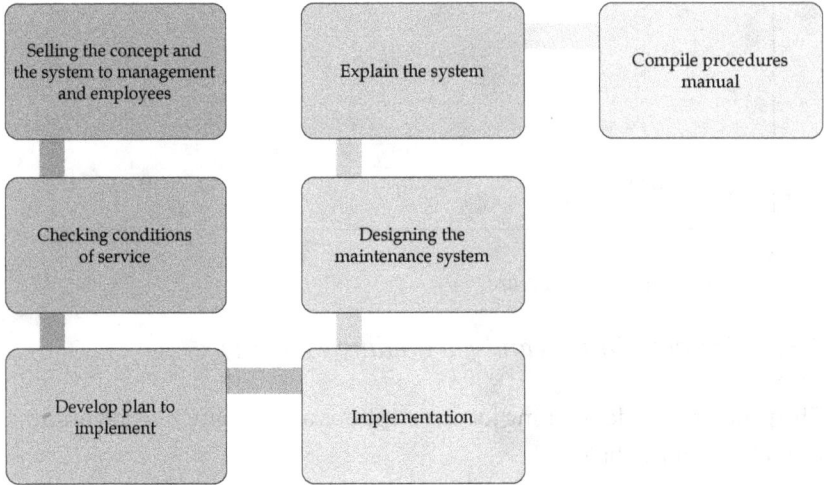

Figure 3.3: Job descriptions and job grading: Stage 2

3.3.3 Comparing stages 1 and 2

The two stages can be compared as shown in Table 3.2 below.

Table 3.2: Comparison of the two stages

Comparing	Stage 1	Stage 2
Flexibility	Inflexible; the grading rules must be applied.	Flexible; individuals can be paid anywhere along the pay scale in line with the organisation pay progression policy.

Comparing	Stage 1	Stage 2
What is taken into account	Looks at the job, not the person performing the job. Grade the JOB and not the PERSON.	Takes account of personal qualities and characteristics of person in job.
Personal or impersonal	Impersonal.	Personal.
What is important	Observe grading rules.	Quality, competence, performance and scarcity of skill and effort are taken into account.

To implement the Job Evaluation process, management should pay special attention to certain guidelines. First, they should be committed to the programme and the motives for carrying it out. Second, they should state their belief in justice and fairness. Third, they should state that no one will have their fixed pay reduced. Fourth, they should reiterate that it is the job that is to be evaluated and not the person. Fifth, they should explain the method simply. Finally, they should ensure appropriate participation. Ignoring these guidelines could lead to failure in the implementation of the Job Evaluation process. Additional elements that may result in a failed Job Evaluation system are now discussed.

3.4 WHY JOB EVALUATION SYSTEMS FAIL

In most cases, where a system collapses, it is not because of the system itself, but is usually due to one of the following factors: weak initial implementation; weak top management support; lack of employee participation and support; upgrading of jobs without a corresponding change of job content; inadequate administrative support; lack of communication; the system not being managed; job descriptions not being reviewed and re-graded as jobs change; new employees and managers not being educated on the system; no cross-correlation of other similar jobs in the organisation leading to inconsistency; and/or lack of transparency.

A job should be re-graded only if there is an appropriate or noticeable change in job responsibilities or in the organisational structure. Resist the temptation to upgrade the job merely so that the person can be paid more – greater flexibility must rather be built into the salary structure. Upgrading without a corresponding change in job content is the major cause of the collapse of Job Evaluation systems.

Having discussed several reasons for the failure of Job Evaluation systems, the next section discusses how to choose a Job Evaluation system so that the system will be most successful in your organisation.

3.5 CHOICE OF A JOB EVALUATION SYSTEM

All currently popular systems produce similar and workable hierarchies. The criteria for the choice of a system are the following: the Chief Executive must understand the system and be committed to it; everyone, including the people at the lowest level in the organisation, must understand and accept the system; the system must be defensible; updating and maintaining the system must not be an administrative burden; the system must be flexible and accommodate all types if grading systems including broad-banding; and the system must be user-friendly and support the culture of the organisation.

There is no such thing as a good or bad Job Evaluation system. They all do the same thing – rank job descriptions relative to one another. Previous studies have shown a 0.94 correlation between all systems of Job Evaluation.[50] Put a different way, it is therefore not entirely unexpected for there to be about 6% of jobs that might differ across grading systems. This is pretty good given that we are dealing with social science and people's perceptions. The next section will discuss how different Job Evaluation systems are categorised.

3.5.1 *Categorisation of Job Evaluation systems*

It is the corruption of a system that makes it seem poor or inappropriate, making maximum participation and commitment essential. Job evaluation systems can be categorised according to the below:

- The basis or method of comparison:

    o   comparing job against job; or

    o   comparing job against some scale.

- The means or method of analysis used:

    o   considering the entire job; or

    o   considering job elements or factors.

Table 3.3: Summary of the various approaches to categorisation of some Job Evaluation systems

Basis or method of comparison		Means or method of analysis	
		Consider job elements or factors	**Consider entire job**
Basis or method of comparison	Comparing job against job	Factor comparison, for example, HAY, IPE	Ranking, internal benchmarking, paired comparisons, market pricing
	Comparing job against some scale	Points methods, for example, Peromnes, JE Manager, EQUATE, JE Paterson Points	Classification methods, for example, Stratified Systems Theory (SST), Paterson, TASK

There are various other considerations to be taken into account when performing a Job Evaluation, which will now be discussed.

3.6 POINTS TO REMEMBER WHEN EVALUATING JOBS

When evaluating jobs, remember the following:

- There is no such thing as a scientific method of Job Evaluation. Although scientific principles and processes may have been used in the development of certain methods, in practice they are all systematic approaches to the establishment of the hierarchy of jobs in an organisation.

- Virtually all Job Evaluation methods used world-wide do the same thing: rank the relative worth of one job to another and produce nearly identical hierarchies.

- Each method has advantages and disadvantages. Organisations should select the best suited according to their requirements but realise that good implementation and ongoing management are more important than the system chosen.

Because there is no such thing as a scientific system of Job Evaluation and because all methods are systematic approaches to grading jobs, the grading committee should be a standing committee, as there are often ongoing appeals to re-evaluate when job content changes and the need to evaluate new jobs.

Finally, a Job Evaluation system must be flexible and grow with an organisation's needs. If it is perceived to be a dynamic, living system, it can even become a motivational influence. There should be procedures for updating job descriptions and subsequent re-evaluations.

3.7 JOB EVALUATION: FREQUENTLY ASKED QUESTIONS AND SAMPLE ANSWERS

Table 3.4 illustrates commonly asked questions from employees about the Job Evaluation process, and some possible answers to these queries.

Table 3.4: Commonly asked questions and possible answers

Commonly Asked Questions	Possible Answers
Am I being evaluated?	Definitely not. The job is being graded regardless of incumbent.
What method of Job Evaluation are we using?	The XYZ method, which is one of the most commonly used systems. It has the following features...

Commonly Asked Questions	Possible Answers
Who will be doing the job grading?	An objective outside consultant or grading committee will receive the job description, with no name on the job description, and apply the grading rules to arrive at an accurate grade.
When are jobs graded?	Jobs are graded whenever there is a significant change in job content, or for new jobs.
Will the company pay me more money as a result of the Job Evaluation?	No. Job evaluation is a process of ranking the relative worth of one job to another. If the job is upgraded, a higher pay scale will apply, but it does not automatically guarantee a pay increase.
Will Job Evaluation solve problems I have with my manager?	Not likely. It does not solve all problems and does not replace good management and leadership.
Why are we implementing Job Evaluation, then?	The organisation needs to have a defensible rationale for developing pay structures to ensure that similar jobs have the same pay range. It is also used to support recruitment processes, organisation design, and facilitating external comparisons of job and pay levels.
Can I see my grade?	Yes, you will be told your grade and it will be explained to you (depending on the organisational policy).
Can I see another person's grade?	No, we respect the individual's right to privacy regarding their remuneration and grade.
What if I do not understand why I am on a particular grade?	First ask your manager or head of department to explain it to you. If there is still uncertainty, speak to the HR manager.
Is there going to be any training?	If there is a need, there will be annual refresher courses on how the system works.

Commonly Asked Questions	Possible Answers
Does the Executive Committee support the principles of Job Evaluation, and are they committed to its fair application?	Yes. EXCO is committed to the fair application of Job Evaluation. To this end, an objective, external consultant will be used to ensure the integrity of the system, either to audit results or to evaluate jobs.
Will my job description and grade put me in a "box" and stifle my creativity?	No, you can be as creative as you can and want. If your role changes because of it, we can re-write your job description to include these changes and re-evaluate the job to determine if your pay grade should also change.
Is Job Evaluation causing too much hierarchy and one-to-one reporting?	Job evaluation per se does not cause this; changes in the organisation design do.

3.8 CONCLUSION

Job evaluation is the systematic and objective process of comparing one job to another within an organisation to arrive at different job levels. It does so without looking at individual characteristics, personalities or performance. All Job Evaluation systems do the same thing, i.e., rank jobs according to complexity of work. Job evaluation systems assist with ensuring equal pay for work of equal value. Many organisations have started to outsource the grading of their job descriptions to keep it professional and impartial. Job evaluation fails when jobs are upgraded without a corresponding change of job content. Job evaluation systems need to be maintained and audits should be done every few years to secure the integrity of the system. Make sure that all leaders have a good understanding of the system you have chosen.

In conclusion, this chapter has provided insight as to the what, why and how of Job Evaluation. It began by discussing what Job Evaluation is and how it came about. It then went on to discuss why Job Evaluation is used, as well as the benefits of its presence and the cons of a lack of presence. Finally, the chapter discussed how to determine the best Job Evaluation system and process for your organisation.

CHAPTER 4

Paterson Job Evaluation

4.1 OVERVIEW AND INTRODUCTION

The Paterson method of Job Evaluation has been implemented in many countries across the world. South African Government reporting is done using Paterson, which makes it one of the most commonly used systems in Africa.

The method contends that jobs, regardless of level, industry or country, can be compared by looking at the kind and complexity of decisions that must be made by an employee. Paterson claims that an organisation's pay structure should reflect the job structure and levels of responsibility that result from Job Evaluation.

The goal of this chapter is to outline the Paterson model and discuss its practical applications. In our view, it is the most suitable system for any organisation because it is flexible enough to accommodate any organisational design (OD) structure, it is easy to understand, is quick to implement and is very robust.

4.1.1 *Key features of the Paterson system*

The Paterson system include concepts and rules developed by Professor Thomas Thomson Paterson in Scotland in 1963. These have been refined over the years to suit the modern world of work, establishing decision-making or freedom to act in a role. In our view, Elliott Jaques' Stratified Systems Theory (SST) is a close cousin to Paterson's theory. Key features of the Paterson system include the below:

- *Non-discriminatory* – no regard for race, gender, religion or creed.

- *International system* – Recognised by ILO (International Labour Organisation).

- Easily *accommodates* broad-banding and multi-skilling.

- Ties in well with the *employment equity* levels.

- A *useful OD* framework and tool.

- *Easy to understand* and communicate.

- *Quick* to implement.

- Supported by *salary surveys.*

4.2 HOW TO CARRY OUT PATERSON JOB EVALUATION

The procedure for Paterson evaluation is as follows:

Table 4.1: Process of grading

Step	Action
1	Band all the job profiles A to F using the rules provided.
2	Sub bands into 'upper' and 'lower' based on the coordination of work in the same band or continuum of skills. This can also be done using sapiential authority.
3	Sub-grade the jobs using the following factors: • Variety • Complexity • Precision • Physical effort/pressure with the qualifiers of education, training time and competence required.

4.3 HIERARCHY OF SKILLS AND DECISIONS

In his original books, Paterson set out the hierarchy of skills and decisions seen in Table 4.2. This is sometimes referred to as classical Paterson with 28 levels. Since then, several versions have evolved, including only having six broad bands and having 11 sub-bands. Very detailed grading rules are not provided in this textbook, but when understood and followed closely, lead to accurate grading.

Table 4.2: Classical Paterson Hierarchy of Skills

BAND	SUB – BAND	SUB – GRADE	DESCRIPTION
F	F Upper	F4, F5	*Co-ordinating or Supervisory (Top Policy)*
	F Lower	F1, F2, F3	*Top Policy*
E	E Upper	E4, E5	*Co-ordinating or Supervisory (Programming)*
	E Lower	E1, E2, E3	*Programming/Long Term*
D	D Upper	D4, D5	*Supervisory (Interpretive)*
	D Lower	D1, D2, D3	*Interpretive/ Probabilistic*
C	C Upper	C4, C5	*Supervisory (Skilled)*
	C Lower	C1, C2, C3	*Routine/Skilled Operational*
B	B Upper	B4, B5	*Supervisory (Semi-Skilled)*
	B Lower	B1, B2, B3	*Operational*
A	A	A1, A2, A3	*Defined*

It is important to take note that the number of tasks will not change a role from an A Band to a B Band, i.e., it does not follow that the longer the job description, the higher the grade. Volume also does not change a grade, for example, if one serves 50 cups of tea a day or 100 cups of tea a day, it does not make the grade go up. Rather, complexity, accountability, decision-making, impact and skills and knowledge can have an impact on changing a band. Therefore, a job profile needs to be comprehensive and detailed enough so that you can discern at what level the role operates, i.e., is it tasks, operations, processes, disciplines (interpretative in nature), programming, or policy-making and defining the strategic intent?

The table below is known as the Banding Clues Table, which may assist in determining the band for a position.

Table 4.3: Banding clues

BAND	LEVEL/TITLE
F	Organisation/s
E	Major Corporate Function/s
D	Discipline/s or Function/s
C	Process/es or system/s
B	Operation/s
A	Task/s

4.4 THE STEPS TO FOLLOW WHEN CONDUCTING A PATERSON JOB EVALUATION

Using the Job Evaluation rules, place each job description in a band (step 1). The factors to be used are predominantly the *types of decisions or decision-making role of the job.*

In order to be able to differentiate between jobs and to grade fairly, one often cannot simply grade a job as a whole, i.e., it may be necessary to *first grade each key task in the job.* **This allows one to establish the highest graded task in the job.** Provided this is done regularly, that should be the grade given to the whole job. In addition, when one is comparing two jobs, it may well be necessary to compare by a count of the number of higher graded tasks.

Since banding is based on the decision-making factor, grades will be allotted mainly in terms of the *level of judgement* each output requires. Factors such as training, supervision required, consequence of errors and pressure of work are also important, but are more a qualification (fine tuning) of the judgement aspect.

If two workers in the same job have different performance or proficiency levels, the grade of the job will be the same, i.e., it is not affected by the "person factor" of performance. Performance is not a grade issue. *Remember you are only looking at the outputs and competencies themselves, and not performance in the job or the person doing the job.*

Step 2 is sub-banding, where you place jobs into the upper or lower section of the band based on whether an employee supervises work in the same level as themselves or not. Continuum of skills and sapiential authority is also sometimes used to place jobs in an upper band. Sapiential authority is a level of wisdom that one acquires over a long period of time. It places a person in the unique position of having an authority that if one did not adhere to, the consequences would be dire and collateral damage too much for the organisation to bear.

4.4.1 *Step 3: Sub-grading of jobs*

The process of sub-grading takes place *one band at a time, starting with A band jobs. Jobs in the same band are compared to each other* in terms of the major criteria, namely:

- variety of tasks;
- complexity of tasks;
- precision; and
- mental or physical effort.

Note: Qualifiers like skill levels and type, education and time taken to learn the job may also be used.

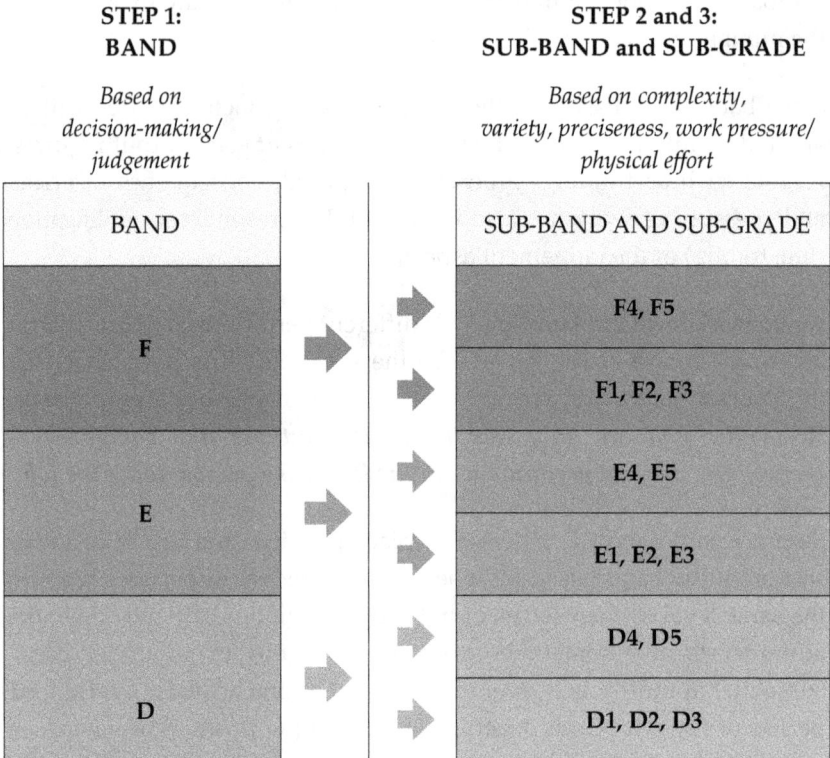

STEP 1: BAND	STEP 2 and 3: SUB-BAND and SUB-GRADE
Based on decision-making/ judgement	*Based on complexity, variety, preciseness, work pressure/ physical effort*

BAND		SUB-BAND AND SUB-GRADE
F	➡ ➡	F4, F5
		F1, F2, F3
E	➡ ➡	E4, E5
		E1, E2, E3
D	➡ ➡	D4, D5
		D1, D2, D3

STEP 1: BAND *Based on decision-making/ judgement*		STEP 2 and 3: SUB-BAND and SUB-GRADE *Based on complexity, variety, preciseness, work pressure/ physical effort*
BAND		**SUB-BAND AND SUB-GRADE**
	⇨	**C4, C5**
C	⇨	**C1, C2, C3**
	⇨	**B4, B5**
B	⇨	**B1, B2, B3**
A		**A1, A2, A3**

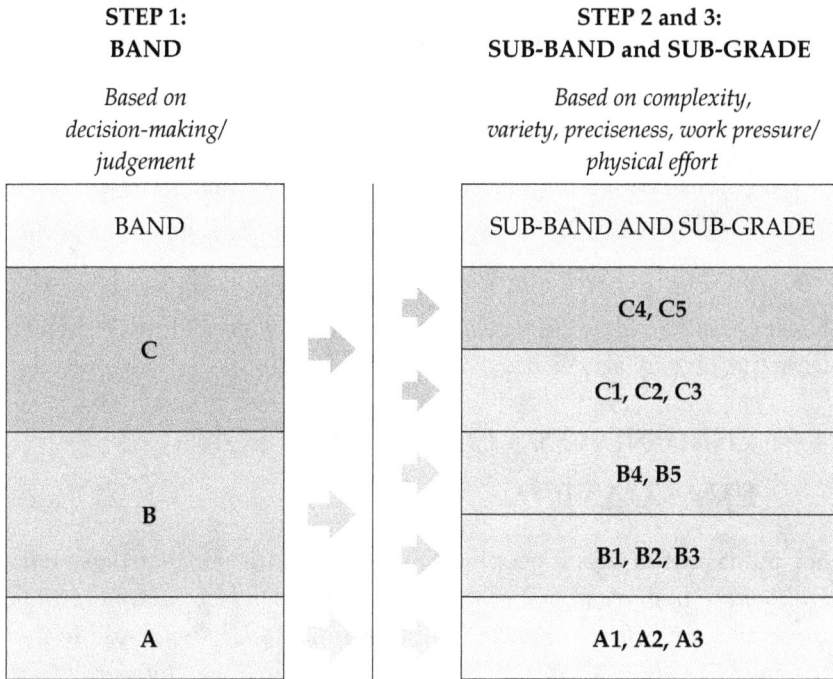

Figure 4.1: Steps used to grade a job

4.5 DEFINITIONS

- *Variety* of tasks:

  o Jobs having a wider variety of tasks are sub-graded higher than jobs where there is little variety.

- *Complexity* of tasks:

  o Jobs having more complex tasks or more complex combinations of tasks are sub-graded higher than those with fewer complex jobs.

  o Where jobs have a larger number of decisions in the same band they are sub-graded higher.

- *Precision*:

  o Jobs requiring a high degree of precision and very strict tolerances are sub-graded higher than jobs where precision is not critical and where tolerances are gross, e.g., an instrument maker or a millwright may be sub-graded higher than a boilermaker.

- *Pressure* of work/physical effort:

  o Jobs demanding high physical and/or mental stress are often sub-graded higher than jobs where these factors are less demanding.

Note: Qualifiers like skill levels and type, education and time taken to learn the job may also be used.

4.6 DIMENSIONS OF A PATERSON JOB EVALUATION

For thousands of years, people have considered it fair that *those who make more important and more difficult decisions be paid more than those who make less important and less difficult decisions*. Add to this the ability to grade all jobs in the same way against the kinds or weight of decisions made, and you have a basis for a simple, fair Job Evaluation method. Paterson defined *six types of decisions or levels of work*, which are found in any organisation. Any job can be defined in terms of these *bands of decision and the authoritative relationships* involved.

Each job is composed of *outputs and competencies*, and the decisions required to complete each can be identified.

4.6.1 *Broad Paterson Bands*

The six types of decisions, called bands or levels of work, can be defined as follows:

Table 4.4: Paterson broad bands

BAND	LEVEL/TITLE	KIND OF DECISION
F	**LEVEL 6** **Policy-making Decisions** (*Top management*)	• Overall policy decisions are regarded as being superior to any other decisions. They are associated with top-level management and give the overall direction of the organisation. • The limits are very wide and in many cases are only specified by the laws of the land. • Top management decides on policy in all major areas of operation (e.g. finance, production, marketing and human resources).
E	**LEVEL 5** **Programming Decisions/Long Term Strategy/ Strategy Execution** (*Senior/General management*)	• The execution of policy is broadly planned or programmed within the limits of discretion set by top management. • Senior management decides on organisation structures. • The overall programme for major functions, the relationship between major functions and the major operation objectives.
D	**LEVEL 4** **Interpretive/ Probabilistic Decisions** (*Middle management/ Professional/ Advanced Specialist*)	• The limits of discretion for interpretive decisions are set by senior management's programme, plan or budget. • The interpretive aspect comes from the choice of a best decision out of a spectrum of possible decisions within the limits of discretion. • These decisions often involve determining the best use of available manpower and machines to achieve the targets agreed in the programme. • Middle management decides on systems and procedures, rules and regulations, plant manuals, localisation plans/ programmes and interpretations not covered by existing rules that is "what to do".

BAND	LEVEL/TITLE	KIND OF DECISION
C	LEVEL 3 Deterministic/ Process /System Decisions (Skilled/ Advanced Operational/ Specialist)	• Once the rules have been set by the interpretive decisions, execution begins. • What is to be done has already been decided and the next level of decision – is the choice of the way in which it is to be carried out from established processes, practice, systems, trade knowledge and rules and regulations. • People taking these decisions can decide which process to use. They know the theory behind the operations. • They must decide "how", "where" and "when".
B	LEVEL 2 Operational/ Subsystem (Semi-skilled/ Operational)	• This is work in which the processes are defined and freedom of choice is restricted to the operations. • Within the constraints of the process – the "how" – the workers can decide "where" and "when" to carry out the operation/s that constitutes the process.
A	LEVEL 1 Defined Decisions (Basic skills)	• The decisions made by the worker can be defined and the worker is left with little choice other than variation in control of the elements of an operation that is "when".

Except for Band A, all bands can be sub-divided into two sub-bands, an upper (U) and a lower (L). This is done because at all these decision levels there are positions where the person must supervise or coordinate the work of other people and jobs in the same Band. Table 4.5 indicates the basic breakdown of the decision structure of an organisation.

Note: However, a person will usually make decisions of lower bands in addition to decisions in the band in which his/her job is located.

Table 4.5: Example of generic job structure by band

BAND	KIND OF DECISION	TITLE/ LEVEL	SUB-BAND	KIND OF GRADE	INDICATIVE TITLES
F	Policy-making Strategic Intent	Top management	F Upper	Co-ordinating or Supervisory (Policy)	Group CEO/ Managing Director
			F Lower	Policy	Executive Director
E	Programming/ Long Term Strategy/ Strategy Execution	Senior/ General management	E Upper	Co-ordinating or Supervisory (Programming)	General Manager Business Manager
			E Lower	Programming/ Long-term	Assistant General Manager Business Area Manager
D	Interpretive/ Probabilistic	Middle management/ Professional/ Advanced Specialist	D Upper	Supervisory (Interpretive)	Department Manager
			D Lower	Interpretive/ Probabilistic	Section Manager
C	Process/ System	Skilled/ Advanced Operational/ Specialist	C Upper	Supervisory (Skilled)	Supervisor Foreman
			C Lower	Process/System	Artisan Chemist Sales Rep
B	Automatic/ Operative/ Subsystem	Semi-skilled/ Operational	B Upper	Supervisory (Semi-Skilled)	Chargehand Bookkeeper
			B Lower	Operative/ Sub-system	Operator Driver Clerical
A	Defined	Basic skills	A	Defined	Trainee Basic Skills

The grades can be further sub-divided into sub-grades. These can be judged by the variety; stress complexity; precision; supervision required; and the skill levels indicated by education, training and experience, of the job.

Important: *At the beginning of a Job Evaluation exercise you will have no idea of the total number of sub-grades required, but you should aim to limit them to the minimum needed by the organisation.* ***It is only possible to establish the total number of sub-grades once all the jobs have been graded and compared with each other at the review sessions.***

For new or first time implementations, one can, to some extent, decide in advance how many levels there should be, but one should let the process unfold.

Role of the Job Evaluation Committee

The role of the Role Evaluation Committee is to:

- appreciate the degree and extent to which jobs add strategic value to the organisation (this is based on the committee's expertise in Job Evaluation and the specific system used;
- understand the strategy and culture of the business (current and future); and
- understand management philosophy, policy and practices.

The Job Evaluation Committee should meet on an ongoing basis and should consist of:

- employees – to be invited to participate when the job profile is ambiguous and needs further clarity by the incumbent;
- members – to represent functional diversity;
- Chairperson – to chair Job Evaluation meetings;
- external consultant/facilitator – to facilitate the committee and ensure grading rules are adhered to (this would ideally become an internal facilitator, e.g., HR Executive/representative);
- alternate members – to participate in the committee in the absence of a member;
- labour representation – to be included in grading jobs within the bargaining unit; and
- secretary – to coordinate meeting requirements and act as a scribe.

4.6.2   Dispute Resolution

Dispute resolution refers to an internal process among the Job Evaluation committee to discuss the grade and gain consensus as a committee. It is important to gain consensus through discussion and consider the evidence in the job profile, and not to rely on voting. Sometimes this is not possible, however, so to resolve the impasse, most organisations follow the steps below:

- *Step 1* – 100% consensus

- *Step 2* – Pending/Problem File/Parking Lot

- *Step 3* – Mediation

- *Step 4* – Arbitration

Management's role: addressing common misconceptions

- Be committed to the concept, system and project.

- State belief in justice and fairness.

- State that no-one's basic pay will be reduced.

- State that the job is to be evaluated, not the person.

- Explain the method simply.

- Ensure maximum participation.

4.6.3   Typical Career Path

Below is an example of a typical dual career path for pay. It illustrates the Paterson Levels for Management and for Specialists, and their respective Paterson grades. Career progression could happen at virtually any level; it is specific to each organisation and the organisation's strategy in terms of career progression and succession planning.

Paterson Level	MANAGEMENT	SPECIALIST	
F 1-5	Top Management	Manager of Technology	*Technology Strategist. Strategic Management of Technology*
E 1-5	Senior Management	Principal Specialist	*Organisational expert within a discipline. Advanced research*
D 1-5	Middle Management	Senior Specialist	*Specialisation within a sub-field of a broad discipline and entry level research*
C 3-5	First Line Supervisor	Specialists	*Specialisation within a broad functional/technical discipline*
C 1-2	Advanced Operational		
B 4-5	Operational Skills		
B 2-3	Auxiliary		

Figure 4.2: Typical career path

4.6.4   Paterson Points

Many countries have legislation on equal pay for work of equal value. 21st Century designed the Paterson Points system based on the defined factors in all countries' legislation to allow us to evaluate and grade jobs based on five major factors, which gave rise to JEasy Paterson Points.

4.6.5   JEasy Paterson Points Job Evaluation Tool

JEasy Paterson Points is a sophisticated, flexible, completely secure, web-based Job Evaluation Point System. Each factor is assigned a weight or points according to how much of that particular factor is present in the job. The more points assigned to a job the more worth the job has to the organisation. This is called the Points Factor Job Evaluation method. It was specifically designed to accommodate an agile workplace and the concept of WFA (work from anywhere). Indeed, even the job grading panel can be sitting anywhere in the world, whilst simultaneously grading a job. A comprehensive audit trail of who graded which job and which level they chose for each factor is stored and used for audit and comparison purposes later should the job have changed.

Table 4.6: Five major factors that encapsulate the Paterson Derived Grading Theory

Skill	Effort	Responsibility
Knowledge and Skills (KS)	Problem Solving (PS)	Judgement (J)
		Accountability (A)
		Impact (I)

This system is state-of-the-art and complies with all labour legislation and the International Labour Organisation's (ILO) standards. In order to use the system responsibly and effectively, it is essential to have a **good working knowledge** and understanding of the **JEasy Paterson Points Job Evaluation system**. For this reason, **Job Evaluation training is included in the price** of the product.

JEasy Paterson Points statements are **available in five languages** – English, Afrikaans, isiXhosa, Sesotho and isiZulu – which 21st Century believes will add credibility to the system.

The next chapter covers the impact of Job Evaluation on salary structures.

CHAPTER 5

The impact of Job Evaluation on salary structures

5.1 INTRODUCTION

Job evaluation can be viewed as a transactional process, with an outcome that merely results in a score, however that only accesses a tiny portion of the value that a Job Evaluation result gives. Job profiling and the resulting Job Evaluation are the cornerstone of all remuneration processes and outcomes, with reward strategy in turn having a direct impact on driving the behaviour needed for organisational success and sustainability. In general, the process of developing a Job Evaluation to meet the organisation's aims is illustrated in Figure 5.1 below.

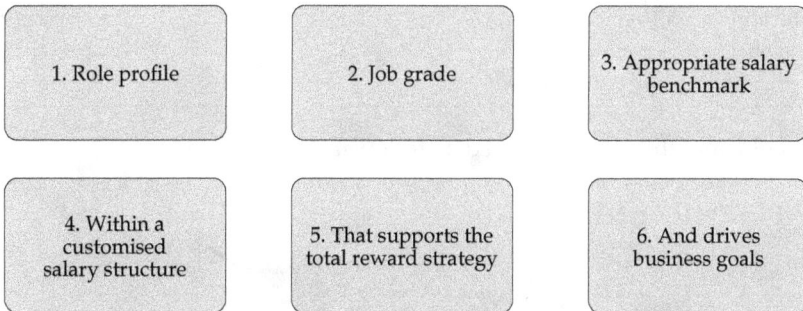

1. Role profile	2. Job grade	3. Appropriate salary benchmark
4. Within a customised salary structure	5. That supports the total reward strategy	6. And drives business goals

Figure 5.1: Process from developing a role to achieving business goals

Job evaluation is an **enabler** in an organisation. This chapter focuses on the design of salary structures, as well as the link between the Job Evaluation process and results to a customised salary structure, beginning with a breakdown of what a salary structure is.

5.2 WHAT IS A SALARY STRUCTURE?

A salary structure serves as a guide for all pay-related decisions. It is also referred to as a pay scale, or a salary scale. A pay structure is a tool designed to create pay levels and pay opportunities that are internally fair, externally competitive and cost-effective. Salary structures are created and administered to support an organisation's pay strategy. A salary structure is unique to an organisation because it speaks to that organisation's bespoke structures, such as its total reward strategy, affordability, the external market the organisation compares against, and the unique business critical skills that are found within the organisation.

A pay structure comprises grades (for example Paterson A, B, C, D, E and F) that have pay ranges attached to them (see Table 5.1).

Table 5.1: Pay structure based on Paterson

Paterson Grade	Pay Range				
	Minimum	Lower Guide	Midpoint	Upper Guide	Maximum
A	A range is created from min to max, around the midpoint		Market data is referenced here		A range is created from min to max, around the midpoint
B1					
B2 and so on					

Graphically this can be viewed as follows:

Pay structure design

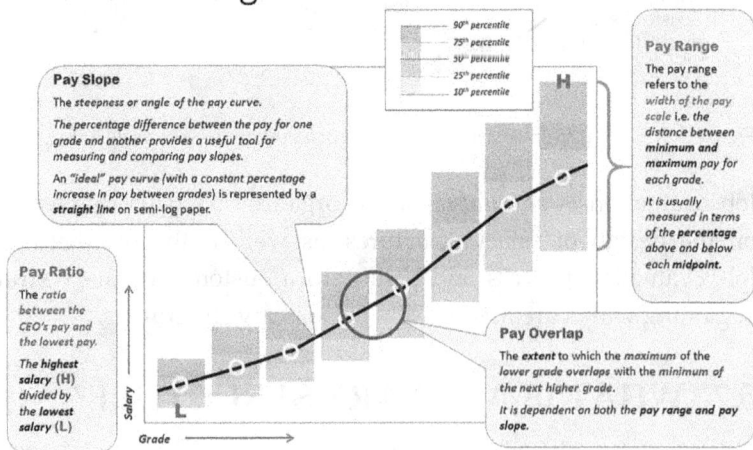

Figure 5.2: Pay structure design with terms defined

Pay structure design demonstrates the link between Job Evaluation and a salary structure. If the grades are incorrect, reference will be made to an incorrect salary reference point. It is clear that in this case, the Job Evaluation result is an important reference point and anchor for the pay structure.

Specifically, pay structures are influenced by supply and demand; the market rate for the job; cost of living; the financial position of the firm or industry; management decisions/policies; trade unions and existing agreements; the current salary/wage structure; the number of grades from top to bottom; and market stance and relativity.

Before designing a pay structure, strategic issues should be considered. These concern whether the structure is able to support the organisation's business strategy; the structure's compatibility with total remuneration design strategy (including fixed and variable remuneration); and the guaranteed pay to variable ratio. Prior to designing a pay structure, additional factors should be considered, such as competitive practices (specifically, external equity); the organisation's job and workplace design approach to produce internal equity (in other words, does the pay structure speak to the organisational structure and the job grade outcomes?); the administrative policies of the organisation; and funds available for pay.

There are a variety of considerations to take into account when designing your pay structure.

Table 5.2: Internal and external equity

Internal equity	External equity
Are the grades correct?	Incorporate relevant market data, with reference to both job content and job grade
Do any job grades look out of place?	Review market inconsistencies and determine importance of market alignment
Does the hierarchy of positions make intuitive sense?	Consider technical design issues

Internal equity	External equity
Is the rater evaluating the job or the person?	
Check peer and subordinate relationships	

Once again, it is the internal equity and Job Evaluation process that must be validated first, so that it speaks accurately to the pay structure that is influenced by the external market.

A salary structure is used for a number of talent management initiatives beyond the salary decision. For example, it can be used for recruitment, performance-related pay decisions, recognition of competence and skill acquisition, career management and pay progression, and differentiation for critical and business imperative skills. The next section considers what informs the salary structure.

5.3 WHAT INFORMS A SALARY STRUCTURE?

Robust salary benchmark information forms the core source of information that sits behind a salary structure. It is thus important to be confident of the salary survey benchmark data, and to be sure that it is relevant. Relevance is important on a number of levels: Are the job matches relevant to the jobs in my organisation? Are we comparing to a relevant sample? Is the data current? Should I age the data to be relevant for the full annual period that my salary structure defines? Is the data specific to the same components of pay we have in our organisation? These are all important conversations that need to happen in choosing the relevant salary survey source for the design of your salary structure.

In diagrammatic format, the components can be represented as shown below. You need to be sure that you are comparing apples with apples if you have offices and divisions in different countries, as an example, and are using different salary surveys. The benefit structures and definitions vary across countries and organisations, and we recommend that you clarify the components your survey is reporting on so that you have a relevant comparison to your own structure.

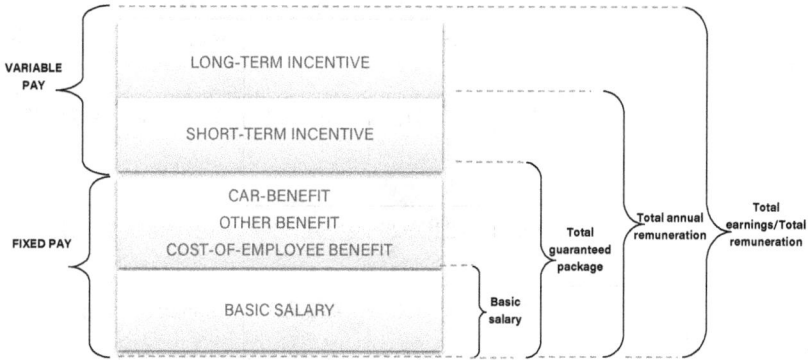

Figure 5.3: Salary structure diagram

In choosing a salary survey you can trust with confidence, consider whether the survey is audited by an independent party, who the survey participants are, whether you can narrow down the comparator-base you would like to compare it with (e.g., an industry or region?). Interrogate the survey methodology: Is full payroll data collected or an average pay per job per survey participant? Is data smoothed or excluded? How often is the data updated? Is the survey a live view of the market or is it aged annually? When choosing a salary survey you can also consider whether all data percentiles are reported, how jobs are matched, and whether job grades are taken into account on the data submission and job matching.

Table 5.3: Example of salary survey data per annum in any currency

Remuneration/ Compensation Element	10th percentile	25th percentile	50th percentile	75th percentile	90th percentile
Basic Salary	248,175	318,055	388,915	486,155	565,969
Fixed Bonus/13th Cheque	21,540	26,808	32,088	36,618	42,318
Total Base Salary	250,419	330,984	412,058	495,798	575,024
Car Allowance	15,560	49,414	74,772	89,940	102,233
Housing Benefit	9,559	9,564	16,704	37,692	91,766
Professional Fees	692	968	3,887	18,877	22,800
Sundry Benefits	3,783	5,066	10,288	25,054	80,028

Remuneration/ Compensation Element	10th percentile	25th percentile	50th percentile	75th percentile	90th percentile
Pension/ Provident Fund Contribution	21,226	31,418	45,993	60,118	71,975
Medical Contribution	16,704	21,792	34,752	47,307	57,686
Total Guaranteed Package	284,030	375,838	476,721	565,953	672,544
Short-term Incentive	23,397	37,020	50,401	77,699	112,327
Total Annual Remuneration	284,913	378,832	480,705	579,583	707,924

In the example above, each line item of pay is independently calculated. Not every incumbent will receive every element of pay/the same benefit mix as other incumbents in the same job match. As an example, there may be a full sample of 105 incumbents, however only 73 incumbents reported a short-term incentive. The percentiles for the short-term incentive are calculated only for the 73 incumbents, resulting in smaller differences between the elements of pay, i.e., Total Guaranteed Package and Total Annual Remuneration. For this reason, the percentiles do not add up mathematically down the columns. In South Africa, the **total guaranteed package benchmark** is the most reliable anchor to compare against, as it includes all guaranteed elements of pay, irrespective of the splits or breakdown. It would be important to choose a relevant focus point per country you are managing.

Remuneration of CEO and Executive positions is more complex, because there is a differentiation of both job grade and remuneration based on the size and complexity of the organisation that the Executive is leading. As the start point, there is not one job grade applicable to all CEOs, CFOs or COOs, as examples. There is certainly relativity between the roles and the layers of leadership, depending on the role that the person assumes, however the size and complexity have the most impact on the job grade. Once the grade is established, one can then compare it in the external market with CEOs of a similar job grade. In terms of salary structuring this is important, because the CEO benchmark becomes the maximum anchor at the midpoint at the top of the pay scale/salary structure, and the relativity flows from that point. Some examples used to determine size and complexity within an organisation are revenue, capital employed, total assets, employee count, number of core businesses, number of operations/branches, number of countries and organisation structure, e.g., holding company/stand-alone/subsidiary/listed or unlisted.

In selecting a relevant external benchmark, organisations would consider to whom they lose skills, and from whom they recruit. It may well be that there are certain skills in an organisation that are more portable, and others that are very niche. In this case, more than one data source is important. Herewith some examples of benchmark considerations of selecting comparators for different reasons: complexity and type (for example, single or multiple product, processes, capital or labour-intensive); market or customer (who do you compete with for share of purse?); organisation structure (for example, another organisation with two large, dominant divisions); location of business (for example, hotels, banks and cell phone companies operate throughout Africa); ownership structure (for example, global owners or family-owned listings); geographic location (it may be relevant to compare with organisations in the region, even though they are not in your industry sector, competing for the same resources or customers – operating a business model).

The preferred trend is to reference a survey that includes all relevant data of a full population of employees, rather than skewing the results by excluding certain data or making assumptions with it. From a user point of view, the important element is to ensure that you are familiar with the methodology of the survey you are using to make decisions. We shall now examine the development of a salary structure.

5.4   DEVELOPING A SALARY STRUCTURE

Having considered what informs a salary structure, we now look at the *HOW...*

This section outlines at a high level the key considerations in the design and development of pay structures. Specifically, it aims to achieve:

- internal equity; and

- external competitiveness.

Internal equity refers to the relative grade assigned to different jobs within an organisation. In addition, internal equity assesses how reasonable these grades are. Internal equity can be examined on two levels – horizontally (i.e., between departments) and vertically (i.e., within one department). Internal equity is a key consideration in developing salary structures, not only within a job family but also amongst various job families that have common job grades. As described herein, the job grade becomes the anchor reference point for the salary structure.

External competitiveness is the second consideration in the design of a salary structure. The focus in this area is on external equity and is based on an organisation's need to compete in a free market for products and services. Part of this competition is the management of labour costs – ensuring that the labour force is neither overpaid (leading to a higher cost than necessary for the organisation to provide/produce its product/ service) nor underpaid (possibly leading to a high turnover or labour unrest which could harm productivity). This external competitiveness is addressed through sourcing data for a relevant comparator group via a reputable salary benchmark survey.

Low turnover or a lack of competitors for labour is not an indicator of a lack of competitiveness in an industry or that the remuneration system is working perfectly in the organisation, since turnover could be related to a number of different non pay-related reasons. However, regular and ongoing market referencing should be conducted via external salary surveys in order to keep track of external market practices. Understanding what the market looks like does not mean that one has to follow it blindly, but that one can make an informed decision that best fits your situation and strategic intention. Remember that a salary survey gives you *context* for your decision-making, rather than the irrefutable and only decision. In simplest terms, these two factors define the two axes in your salary structure – as per this diagram it is the grade (internal equity) and salary (external competitiveness):

Pay structure design

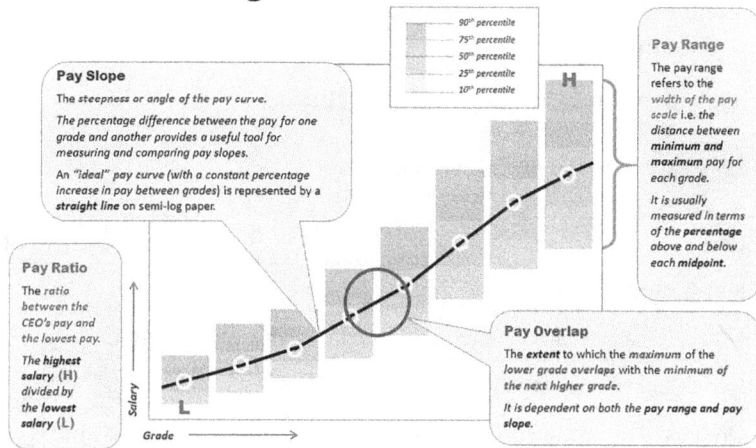

Pay Slope

The *steepness or angle of the pay curve.*

The percentage difference between the pay for one grade and another provides a useful tool for measuring and comparing pay slopes.

An *"ideal" pay curve (with a constant percentage increase in pay between grades) is represented by a* **straight line** on semi-log paper.

Legend:
- 90th percentile
- 75th percentile
- 50th percentile
- 25th percentile
- 10th percentile

Pay Range

The pay range refers to the *width of the pay scale i.e. the distance between* **minimum and maximum** pay for each grade.

It is usually measured in terms of the **percentage** above and below each **midpoint**.

Pay Ratio

The *ratio between the CEO's pay and the lowest pay.*

The **highest salary** (H) divided by the **lowest salary** (L)

Pay Overlap

The **extent** to which the *maximum* of the lower grade overlaps with the *minimum* of the next higher grade.

It is dependent on both the pay range and pay slope.

Figure 5.4: Pay structure Illustrated on a grade scale and a salary scale

Where the two intersect becomes your "playing field" for a pay decision at a certain grade/level. Alongside a salary structure, organisations would likely also have policy guidelines regarding *placement* and *progression* within the pay scale.

Having sourced external salary survey benchmark data, this would typically be used to anchor the midpoint of the salary structure per grade, and the remaining decisions would be related to technical issues, such as:

- the number of points in the pay scale, e.g., three points – minimum, midpoint, maximum;

- the range – the width of the pay scale, i.e., the distance between minimum and maximum pay for each grade;

- the overlap – the extent to which the maximum of the lower grade overlaps with the minimum of the next higher grade, which is dependent on both the pay range and pay slope;

- the distribution of actual current pay to the proposed scale, via comparative ratio analysis, which would determine the number of outliers and the cost to adopt the pay scale; and

- the lead/lag strategy, i.e., do we match to market at the increase month, or six months ahead so that we lead the market for six months and then lag the market for six months, as one example.

Herewith a check-list for implementation.

Table 5.4: Checklist for implementation

Item	Check
Job grading is complete and grades are signed off	
External market salary benchmarks are available for each grade	
Individual salaries are available for each grade	
Organisation remuneration policy and strategy are available and give guidance on design issues such as: • market stance; • guaranteed pay: variable pay philosophy; • performance, contribution and competence pay stance (pay progression principles); and • range, slope, overlap philosophy.	
Cost-benefit analysis of several options is done	
An implementation project plan covering: • timing; • communication plan; • dealing with anomalies (upgrades, downgrades, salaries above and below the proposed pay scales); and • stakeholder presentations, e.g., remuneration committee, EXCO, trade union.	
Policy and procedure document has been written	

5.5 CONCLUSION

In closing, remember the building blocks that lead to the design of a robust salary structure. If you have accurate and up-to-date **role profiles** then you can establish an accurate **job grade**, which enables you to gather appropriate **external market data** that informs a **customised salary structure**. A salary structure is only one part of a total reward strategy that can influence the people you attract, how engaged they are, and whether they stay in your organisation. Do not underestimate how what seems to be an administrative process can be used to influence your organisation and how it grows into the future.

The next chapter uncovers pay for work of equal value. It discusses how the concept came about, with special focus on the pay gap. It further suggests ways in which to close the pay gap to arrive at a more equal society.

CHAPTER 6

Equal pay for work of equal value

6.1 INTRODUCTION

In recent years, the gender pay gap has gained infamy. Starting out
as a noticeable disparity, the gender pay gap concern escalated to an
outcry of unfairness when the 2018 #MeToo Movement exploded onto
the scene. The #MeToo Movement was initiated in retaliation to gender-
based violence and spilt over into the workplace, raising awareness of the
oppression women experience by being paid less when doing the same
work as men, by being denied promotional opportunities or the chance
to occupy leadership roles in proportion to men, and for treatment they
felt was unacceptable.

The gender pay gap has become a serious concern for organisations
far and wide, as women are slowly beginning to combat the disparity
by filing class action lawsuits. Oracle Corp., an American computer
technology corporation, was recently made an example of when three
female employees won the right to represent a body of over 4,000 of their
own. It was alleged that Oracle Corp. paid men more than women for
work considerably similar in terms of responsibility, effort and skill, as
well as working conditions. The pay disparity could not be accounted
for by experience, education, tenure and the performance management
system. The U.S. Labour Department has held Oracle Corp. accountable
for $400 million owed to minority groups and women. The International
Labour Organisation reported the global average of the pay gap to be
20%[51], and despite the gender pay gap reducing each year, the amount
is incremental.

Pay inequity not only pertains to gender, but extends to minority
groups such as those from diverse ethnic backgrounds and those with
disabilities. Inequity could exist between an organisation's internal
employees and those they outsource, part-time workers and full-time
employees, and even temporary and permanent employees.

In the US, only a third (35%) of individuals living with disabilities are employed. This unemployment rate is high, seeing that the majority (76%) of non-disabled individuals are employed.[52] This disparity grows continually. Similarly, European Union countries have reported an employment rate of 47% of those with disabilities and 67% for those without.[53] Even when disabled individuals do have a job, they may be employed in unfavourable circumstances, such as having to do part-time work, receiving below average wages, or being forced to work fewer hours (and thus, receiving less pay).[54] In creating an equal and fair society, these societal norms need to be addressed. Equal pay for work of equal value is thus at the forefront of an equal society.

6.2 EQUAL PAY FOR WORK OF EQUAL VALUE

Equal pay for work of equal value (herein referred to as equal pay), pertains to the right of all genders to receive the same payment for the same work. If women receive less than men for work that is the same or similar in nature, proof must be provided by the employer that the discrepancy is owed to a factor other than gender. This is purely a gender-based example – a number of discriminatory factors would be considered indefensible.

The UK provides a model for equal pay legislation that other countries may use as a baseline for gender-based solutions, i.e., all genders have the right to be paid the same for work that is alike, is deemed equivalent via Job Evaluation, or is of equal value.

The above points are defined as follows:

- **Work that is alike**: Work performed by two or more employees who are in the same, or similar, roles.

- **Work that is deemed equivalent**: Work performed by two or more individuals which has received the same rating as per a Job Evaluation system, despite the fact that the two or more employees performing the work have entirely different jobs.

- **Work of equal value:** Work that requires a similar skill and ability level, despite the jobs of two or more of the employees performing the work being very different.

If the comparison of work is so simple, how did the gender pay gap emerge in the first place?

6.2.1 *How did the pay gap emerge?*

The gender pay gap largely emerged from societal norms. Historically, men were the breadwinners, thus jobs that were perceived to need a man's hand assumed higher value. Women were given the role of caring for children and thus veered to part-time work while doing so. Women also had to forfeit promotional opportunities as their dual-purpose lifestyle (part-time work and caring for children) hindered their working life. The modern day has paved the way for a more diluted gap between gender roles. Females take on what were considered previously male-dominated occupations, and males have transitioned into sharing what was previously seen as a female role (e.g., being granted paternity leave to look after children).

Given the modern workplace demographic and females earning the right to be treated as equal to men, it is evident that they should receive equal pay for their work (if their work is alike, deemed equivalent, or of equal value to those of their male counterparts). However, studies show that this is not the case. A study of Uber rideshare drivers showed that in the US, the average man earned 7% more than the average woman on an hourly basis.[55] A global study on task-based work on an online platform showed that women earned an average of 37% less per hour than men.[56] Palpably, this problem needs to be addressed to eradicate feelings of unfairness on behalf of women and minority groups in the workplace, and to create an equal and fair society.

The pay gap may be caused by discriminatory and non-discriminatory practices. Where discrimination exists, it must be eradicated. The ILO distinguishes between discriminatory and non-discriminatory practices, where discriminatory practices are those mentioned above (where unequal pay is received for work of equal value), and non-discriminatory practices pertain to the differences in treatment between parties, dependant on the requirements of a job. Being male or female may be a logical prerequisite for a job that requires physical performance, for instance, if a country wanted to break a world record for having the fastest person in the world, they would recruit men. It is probably not wrong to say that men generally run faster than women and the 10 fastest people in the world are all men. This is not to say that women do not have their own natural characteristics that allow them to be the best at certain things, for instance, only women (so far) are able to be surrogates.

Essentially, differentiated treatment based on the exigencies of a job is not considered discriminatory, however, when differentiated treatment surpasses the basic necessities of a job, an organisation may want to delve deeper into their practices to determine whether they are being fair to their employees or not. The ILO attributes the existence of the gender pay gap to the following factors:

- **Job type**: Women commonly assume lower-paid careers while men over-represent highly paid careers. Women are commonly associated with part-time work.

- **Productivity characteristics related to gender**: This includes level of education, type of studies, level in the organisation and work experience.

- **Number of hours invested**: Men work more hours than women.

- **Characteristics of organisations of employment**: The type of industry, the size of the organisation and the unionisation will affect the pay gap.

- **Remuneration practices**: These may be conducted in a way that directly or indirectly discriminates. Direct discrimination applies when different pay is accorded to different groups. On the other hand, indirect discrimination crops up when policies and practices used to set pay are tainted. Thus, the *procedures* behind remunerating are discriminatory. Unconscious bias often plagues these procedures. There may be bias in Job Evaluation methods, job classification, and job grading and remuneration systems that disfavour minority groups.

The method used by 21st Century to calculate gender pay gaps is well tried, tested and robust, with consideration of global best practice. Methodologies to calculate these gaps are described in Chapter 7, with detailed consideration of the advantages and disadvantages of each method.

6.2.2 *What are the benefits of closing the pay gap?*

Closing the pay gap is beneficial for society beyond obvious reasons. Of course, obvious reason are the emergence of a fair and equal society, equal pay benefitting the economy. Equal pay promotes the participation of minority groups in the economy and has positive implications thereafter. For those who are already participating in the economy, equal pay encourages their full potential. When individuals believe they are being fairly treated by an organisation, their motivation, productivity and willingness to go over and above to assist an organisation in reaching its goals is likely to increase. When individuals perceive unfairness, the opposite is likely to happen.

Bridging the pay gap may also contribute to an organisation's Corporate Social Responsibility (CSR). Studies show that CSR practices positively influence an organisation's reputation.[57] Furthermore, it is likely that people will be inspired to support organisations they feel do not discriminate against them.

6.2.3 *Misconceptions around the pay gap*

Various parties may be reluctant to close the pay gap due to the misconception that it will be a costly task. However, research by the ILO has shown that closing the pay gap would be easier and less costly than may be presumed. For instance, the ILO shows that the gender pay gap sits at approximately 16% across countries in the European Union, whereas the amount needed to close the pay gap is 1 to 2% of the wage bill. This is because the pay gap is acclaimed to be lower in an organisation than in society in general.

Concerning lower wages for disabled employees, employers argue that it costs them to build the necessary infrastructure in the workplace to accommodate these employees. However, once again, this has been proven incorrect by parties such as the Job Accommodation Network.[58] On the contrary, hiring an individual with a disability outweighs the cost of implementing the infrastructure for them. A study cited by the ILO showed that 65% of Australian employers rated "neutral" when asked about the financial cost of implementing infrastructure for their disabled employees, implying that the cost was not significant enough to affect their financial status. In fact, 20% of Australian employers rated that hiring disabled individuals benefited their organisation financially.

Misconceptions about the cost of hiring disabled individuals means that these individuals are less likely to be hired and are thus an untouched talent pool in the market. This means that an array of talent with skills, education, knowledge and know-how is being neglected. Employees may find that the missing link they have been waiting for is right before their eyes, yet general assumptions about the cost of hiring disabled individuals has created a pay gap.

Having discussed the pay gap and the factors resulting in its emergence, the next section focuses on reversing the gap to achieve a more equal and fair society.

6.3 HOW WILL EMPLOYEES RECTIFY THE CURRENT SITUATION?

For the pay gap to be rectified, it needs to be addressed by stakeholders on a global scale, on a national scale, and on an organisation-wide scale.

6.3.1 *Global scale*

For the pay gap to be addressed globally, society needs to address its own norms and beliefs. Stakeholders also need to become aware of the prevailing inequality, which may be achieved through awareness and education. Technology and social media platforms exist now that allow individuals to have a worldwide awareness, thus gender equality campaigns have the capacity to be spread far and wide, so that various nations receive insight (excluding some countries that are under strong dictatorial rule). This would specifically affect gender-based biases and contribute toward addressing gender-based inequality. The same could be said for any other area of unfair discrimination.

6.3.2 *National scale*

Often, a country needs to go through a state of emergency before any type of change occurs. Civil unrest or interference from other nations may precede change, yet once this has occurred, or if it does not need to occur at all, the stakeholders of a country need to work towards establishing legislation to translate the nation's beliefs into a structured policy. Those who feel that the common belief has not been met may challenge the offender.

Gender pay gap legislation differs dramatically, however basic workplace gender pay gap legislation should stipulate who holds the right to make a claim vis-à-vis equal pay. Legislation in certain countries may, for instance, state that equal pay claims are limited to employees who are required to deliver work, while legislation in other countries may allow a claimant to be a contractor. Gender pay gap legislation should determine when a claimant's rights are being breached, for instance, when equal work performed receives unequal pay. Equal pay legislation should also specify the process of a claim. For example, in the UK, an applicant must identify, before an employment tribunal, an individual of the opposite gender who is working for the same employer or another employer and performing equal work. This identified individual is called a 'comparator' and must be shown to be paid more, or otherwise have more favourable terms and conditions of employment, than the applicant. The comparator may even be a hypothetical situation.

Legislation may also help bridge the pay gap by making pay audits compulsory in organisations, with companies being obliged to report their figures annually. This allows other stakeholders to determine whether they would like to support these organisations, or work for them.

6.3.3 *Organisation-wide scale*

Fixing a problem that has been around for a very long time but has not been considered a problem may prove to be a challenge. Organisations that have already established their practices are now forced to reshuffle these to accommodate legislation and other stakeholders. Let's face it – who wants to work for, or support, an organisation that violates human rights? It is in the best interests of an organisation to fix any unfair pay gap, whether legislation requires it or not.

The ILO proposed that pay inequity may be addressed by way of one of three different models. The model of choice should be suited to the specific circumstances of the organisation and should be influenced by public policy and the pro-activeness of the employer. The proposed models are as follows:

- **Model 1:** A comprehensive approach with the objective of eradicating discrimination in remuneration practices and discriminatory practices that have resulted in the pay gap.

- **Model 2:** A partial approach with the objective of eradicating discrimination in remuneration practices.

- **Model 3:** A mixed approach with the objective of eradicating particular discriminatory practices and the gender pay gap.

Whether an organisation employs Model 1, Model 2 or Model 3, eradicating discrimination in organisational practices is a common goal. As such, it is important to assess the various forms of discrimination that one may not have previously been conscious of.

The following are steps that organisations may take to close the pay gap throughout the employee life-cycle:

The Attraction Stage

In the attraction stage, where organisations attempt to encourage talent to apply to work for them, organisations must be sure to advertise to candidates who were previously not in their line of sight. These should include minority groups and those who have previously been left out the market. By not doing so, organisations are potentially missing important talent in the market.

The Recruitment Stage

In the recruitment stage, organisations sieve through talent, choosing who is the best fit for the business. Organisations should thus ensure that their recruitment practices are free from bias. Unconscious-bias training may be employed to exclude bias in the recruitment process, and caution should be taken to ensure that the entire process is bias-free. For instance, job descriptions may be phrased in a way that may be deemed negative by certain demographic groups and deter them from wanting to work for the organisation. Thus, job descriptions should be universal and considerate of all groups.

Another way of eliminating bias may be to set the salary for the position, before even knowing who the candidate is. After determining the candidate's experience and educational level, the amount may be adjusted within the formal salary scale. As an employee may attempt to sue their employer for work of equal value attributed to historical differences, employers should not rely on a candidate's salary history when setting pay. Basing a salary on an individual's salary history implies that an employer is relying on the candidate's previous organisation of employment to get it right. What if the previous candidate is worth more than they were previously paid and they are talent that needs to be held onto? What if the previous organisation was discriminatory? Rather than relying on the workings of the previous organisation, an organisation should start afresh, conduct its own audit, and conduct it in an objective, non-biased way. This reinforces the importance of a robust salary scale, as per previous chapters of this book.

Job types, pay structures and Job Evaluation schemes that do not have built-in biases (about skill levels required for jobs, or anything that will discriminate against women or other minority groups) should be utilised for good practice (in light of, for instance, female-related skills and abilities being associated with lesser value on the part of societal norms). Consideration should be made to remain indiscriminate of flexible working hours, part-time work and other positions previously discriminated against.

In the UK, an employee may sue an employer if they are not receiving equal value for equal work. The reason for the difference must not be attributed to a 'material factor', however, which refers to a factor that is non-discriminatory in nature. A material factor may be related to job performance, for instance, and the employer may prove that the difference in compensation between the members of each gender are as per a performance management review.

An employee must not rely on the 'material factor' as it is only applicable if it does not place a member from a disadvantaged group in a position of excessive disadvantage. However, this disproportionate advantage is justifiable in court if it had the purpose of achieving a legitimate aim. An example would be that of a male and female in the same role who perform the same tasks, but the male receives greater compensation owing to his increased experience over that of the female who has taken greater breaks for childcare purposes. Compensating the male more for his greater experience is a justifiable means in most cases.

Here are some steps to close the pay gap in organisations:

- Conduct a pay audit by determining what the company values in pay differentiation and pay progression decisions (e.g., skill, experience, education, tenure, responsibility, risk-level, performance) in relation to the different employee groups (genders, disability, other minority groups). This pay audit should be conducted annually as the organisational composition varies when employees enter and exit. Pay should not only relate to salary, but should include the Total Earnings (fixed and variable pay, per grouping).

- Reverse existing disparities by reviewing employees' pay and comparing it to the market-related norm according to salary surveys. These market-related surveys may be undervaluing female-dominated jobs, as per societal norms. Thus, look towards data collected from female-dominated organisations or boost the value of lower paid jobs. The value of higher paid jobs may be reduced to redirect finances.

- Commit to transparency. Employees should be in the know as to how their pay is determined. This allows them to observe the fairness of the process and establish what factors may allow them to receive a bonus or a higher salary. Building a sense of trust in the salary decision-making process has a big impact on employee engagement and commitment.

- Reward output rather than number of hours. Men often have more hours to dedicate to work while women often have dual roles such as childcare. Rewarding output will motivate employees to perform quicker and produce work of a higher standard, rather than lagging at the office to score higher on the time sheet. This will ensure that within a specific time period, both genders are receiving equal pay.

- The work structure may be altered to accommodate employees, which may serve the organisation in return. Flexible hours and remote working locations may allow employees to put more time into their work that is more suitable for them, resulting in increased productivity for the organisation.

The On-boarding Stage

The on-boarding stage relates to employees' organisational socialisation, where they acquire the behaviour and knowledge of the organisation to help them settle in. The organisational culture is important in this step as it dictates to newcomers what is appropriate behaviour in the organisation and what is not. In eradicating inequality, organisations should create a culture of fairness and respect, displaying that all stakeholders have equal opportunities.

The Development Stage

The development stage of the employee life-cycle pertains to the training and development of the employee. All employees should have equal access to development opportunities.

The Retention Stage

Retention refers to the attempt of the employee to keep talent at their organisation rather than having them seek jobs elsewhere. Retention may also contribute to the gender pay gap as men are more likely to bargain for and attain higher salaries than women as they negotiate between organisations. So as not to increase the gender pay gap, it is important that employers continue to pay equally. A suggestion is that if a male has bartered for a higher salary and this is linked to his performance review, a woman who performs equally on her performance review should be awarded the same.

The Organisational Exit Stage

Organisational exit pertains to an employee who leaves the organisation and is often accompanied by an employee's retirement plan when they decide to stop working. Employers should ensure equality in retirement plans, based on their previous equal pay.

6.4 CONCLUSION

Establishing equal pay for work of equal value may be the act of re-establishing norms or becoming proactive in bridging the pay gap. This requires help from legislation or organisations that want to improve their Corporate Social Responsibility (CSR) or their reputation. However, with more attention paid to the topic, the pay disparity may be addressed and closed to pave the way for an equal society. Although there is still some way to go, South Africa has made great strides and is ranked 18th out of 156 countries when it comes to the gender pay gap. The Global Gender Gap Index benchmarks the evolution of gender-based gaps among four key dimensions (Economic Participation and Opportunity, Educational Attainment, Health and Survival, and Political Empowerment) and tracks progress towards closing these gaps over time. The figure below sets out the rankings of the 156 participating countries.

Having discussed the emergence of the pay gap, Chapter 7 focuses on measuring income inequality.

Table 6.1: The Global Gender Gap Index 2021 Rankings[59]

Rank	Country	Score (0-1)	Rank change 2020	Score change 2020	Score change 2006
1	Iceland	0,892	–	+0,016	+0,111
2	Finland	0,861	1	+0,029	+0,065
3	Norway	0,849	-1	+0,007	+0,050
4	New Zealand	0,840	2	+0,041	+0,089
5	Sweden	0,823	-1	+0,003	+0,009
6	Namibia	0,809	6	+0,025	+0,122
7	Rwanda	0,805	2	+0,014	n/a
8	Lithuania	0,804	25	+0,059	+0,096
9	Ireland	0,800	-2	+0,002	+0,066
10	Switzerland	0,798	8	+0,019	+0,098
11	Germany	0,796	-1	+0,010	+0,044
12	Nicaragua	0,796	-7	-0,008	+0,139
13	Belgium	0,789	14	+0,039	+0,081
14	Spain	0,788	-6	-0,006	+0,056
15	Costa Rica	0,786	-2	+0,003	+0,092
16	France	0,784	-1	+0,003	+0,132
17	Philippines	0,784	-1	+0,003	+0,032
18	South Africa	0,781	-1	+0,001	+0,068
19	Serbia	0,780	20	+0,044	n/a
20	Latvia	0,778	-9	-0,007	+0,069
21	Austria	0,777	13	+0,033	+0,078
22	Portugal	0,775	13	+0,031	+0,083
23	United Kingdom	0,775	-2	+0,008	+0,038
24	Canada	0,772	-5	+0,001	+0,056
25	Albania	0,770	-5	+0,001	+0,109
26	Burundi	0,769	6	+0,024	n/a
27	Barbados	0,769	1	+0,019	n/a
28	Moldova	0,768	-5	+0,011	+0,055
29	Denmark	0,768	-15	-0,014	+0,022
30	United States	0,763	23	+0,039	+0,059
31	Netherlands	0,762	7	+0,026	+0,037
32	Mozambique	0,758	24	+0,035	n/a
33	Belarus	0,758	-4	+0,012	n/a
34	Mexico	0,757	-9	+0,003	+0,111
79	Thailand	0,710	-4	+0,003	+0,027
80	Kazakhstan	0,710	-8	-0,001	+0,017
81	Russian Federation	0,708	–	+0,002	+0,031
82	Tanzania	0,707	-14	-0,006	+0,004
83	Cyprus	0,707	8	+0,015	+0,064
84	Malta	0,703	6	+0,010	+0,051
85	Uruguay	0,702	-48	-0,035	+0,047
86	Paraguay	0,702	14	+0,019	+0,046
87	Viet Nam	0,701	–	+0,002	n/a
88	Romania	0,700	-33	-0,024	+0,020
89	Dominican Republic	0,699	-3	-0,001	+0,035
90	Belize	0,699	20	+0,028	n/a
91	Venezuela	0,699	-24	-0,014	+0,032
92	Lesotho	0,698	-4	+0,003	+0,017
93	Brazil	0,695	-1	+0,004	+0,041
94	Liberia	0,693	3	+0,008	n/a
95	Kenya	0,692	14	+0,021	+0,044
96	Cameroon	0,692	–	+0,006	+0,105
97	Ethiopia	0,691	-15	-0,015	+0,096
98	Greece	0,689	-14	-0,012	+0,035
99	Hungary	0,688	6	+0,011	+0,019
100	Azerbaijan	0,688	-6	+0,001	n/a
101	Indonesia	0,688	-16	-0,013	+0,034
102	Korea, Rep.	0,687	6	+0,016	+0,071
103	Cambodia	0,684	-14	-0,010	+0,055
104	Senegal	0,684	-5	-0,000	n/a
105	Togo	0,683	35	+0,068	n/a
106	Nepal	0,683	-5	+0,003	+0,135
107	China	0,682	-1	+0,006	+0,026
108	Kyrgyz Republic	0,681	-15	-0,007	+0,007
109	Myanmar	0,681	5	+0,016	n/a
110	Mauritius	0,679	5	+0,014	+0,046
111	Brunei Darussalam	0,678	-16	-0,009	n/a
112	Malaysia	0,676	-8	-0,001	+0,026

Rank	Country					
35	Argentina	0,752	0,752	-5	+0,005	+0,069
36	Lao PDR	0,750	0,750	7	+0,019	n/a
37	Trinidad and Tobago	0,749	0,749	-13	-0,007	+0,069
38	Bulgaria	0,746	0,746	11	+0,019	+0,059
39	Cuba	0,746	0,746	-8	+0,000	n/a
40	Jamaica	0,741	0,741	1	+0,006	+0,040
41	Slovenia	0,741	0,741	-5	-0,002	+0,066
42	Ecuador	0,739	0,739	6	+0,011	+0,096
43	El Salvador	0,738	0,738	37	+0,032	+0,055
44	Panama	0,737	0,737	2	+0,007	+0,044
45	Croatia	0,733	0,733	15	+0,013	+0,019
46	Estonia	0,733	0,733	-20	-0,019	+0,038
47	Zimbabwe	0,732	0,732	-	+0,002	+0,086
48	Montenegro	0,732	0,732	23	+0,021	n/a
49	Georgia	0,732	0,732	25	+0,024	+0,061
50	Australia	0,731	0,731	-6	+0,000	+0,015
51	Suriname	0,729	0,729	26	+0,023	n/a
52	Eswatini	0,729	0,729	31	+0,026	+0,069
53	Guyana*	0,728	0,728	n/a	n/a	n/a
54	Singapore	0,727	0,727	-	+0,004	+0,072
55	Luxembourg	0,726	0,726	-4	+0,001	+0,059
56	Zambia	0,726	0,726	-11	-0,005	+0,090
57	Madagascar	0,725	0,725	5	+0,007	+0,087
58	Bahamas	0,725	0,725	3	+0,005	n/a
59	Colombia	0,725	0,725	-37	-0,034	+0,020
60	Israel	0,724	0,724	4	+0,006	+0,035
61	Bolivia	0,722	0,722	-19	-0,012	+0,089
62	Peru	0,721	0,721	4	+0,007	+0,059
63	Italy	0,721	0,721	13	+0,014	+0,075
64	Timor-leste	0,720	0,720	53	+0,058	n/a
65	Bangladesh	0,719	0,719	-15	-0,006	+0,092
66	Uganda	0,717	0,717	-1	-0,000	+0,037
67	Honduras	0,716	0,716	-9	-0,006	+0,068
68	Cape Verde	0,716	0,716	-16	-0,009	n/a
69	Mongolia	0,716	0,716	10	+0,010	+0,034
70	Chile	0,716	0,716	-13	-0,007	+0,070
71	Botswana	0,716	0,716	2	+0,006	+0,026
113	Fiji	0,674	0,674	-10	-0,003	n/a
114	Armenia	0,673	0,673	-16	-0,011	n/a
115	Malawi	0,671	0,671	1	+0,007	+0,027
116	Sri Lanka	0,670	0,670	-14	-0,009	-0,050
117	Ghana	0,666	0,666	-10	-0,007	+0,000
118	Guinea	0,660	0,660	7	+0,018	n/a
119	Angola	0,657	0,657	-1	-0,004	+0,053
120	Japan	0,656	0,656	1	-0,003	+0,011
121	Sierra Leone	0,655	0,655	-10	-0,012	n/a
122	Guatemala	0,655	0,655	-9	-0,011	+0,049
123	Benin	0,653	0,653	-4	-0,004	+0,075
124	Burkina Faso	0,651	0,651	5	-0,016	+0,066
125	Tajikistan	0,650	0,650	12	-0,024	n/a
126	Tunisia	0,649	0,649	-2	+0,005	+0,020
127	Gambia, The	0,644	0,644	9	+0,016	-0,000
128	Maldives	0,642	0,642	-5	-0,004	n/a
129	Egypt	0,639	0,639	5	+0,010	+0,061
130	Bhutan	0,639	0,639	1	+0,004	n/a
131	Jordan	0,638	0,638	7	+0,015	+0,027
132	Lebanon	0,638	0,638	13	+0,038	n/a
133	Turkey	0,638	0,638	-3	-0,003	+0,053
134	Côte d'Ivoire	0,637	0,637	8	+0,030	n/a
135	Papua New Guinea	0,635	0,635	-8	-0,001	n/a
136	Algeria	0,633	0,633	-4	-0,001	+0,031
137	Bahrain	0,632	0,632	-4	-0,003	+0,043
138	Niger*	0,629	0,629	n/a	n/a	n/a
139	Nigeria	0,627	0,627	-11	-0,008	+0,016
140	India	0,625	0,625	-28	-0,042	+0,024
141	Vanuatu	0,625	0,625	-15	-0,013	n/a
142	Qatar	0,624	0,624	-7	-0,005	n/a
143	Kuwait	0,621	0,621	-21	-0,029	-0,013
144	Morocco	0,612	0,612	-1	+0,008	+0,030
145	Oman	0,608	0,608	-1	+0,006	n/a
146	Mauritania	0,606	0,606	-5	-0,008	+0,022
147	Saudi Arabia	0,603	0,603	-1	-0,003	+0,079
148	Chad	0,593	0,593	-1	-0,003	+0,068
149	Mali	0,591	0,591	-10	-0,030	-0,009

72	United Arab Emirates	0,716	0,716	48	+0,060	+0,124
73	North Macedonia	0,715	0,715	-3	+0,004	+0,017
74	Ukraine	0,714	0,714	-15	-0,007	+0,034
75	Poland	0,713	0,713	-35	-0,023	+0,033
76	Bosnia and Herzegovina	0,713	0,713	-7	+0,001	n/a
77	Slovak Republic	0,712	0,712	-14	-0,007	+0,036
78	Czech Republic	0,711	0,711	–	+0,004	+0,039

150	Iran, Islamic Rep.	0,582	0,582	-2	-0,002	+0,002
151	Congo, Democratic Rep.	0,576	0,576	-2	-0,002	n/a
152	Syria	0,568	0,568	-2	-0,001	n/a
153	Pakistan	0,556	0,556	-2	-0,007	+0,013
154	Iraq	0,535	0,535	-2	+0,005	n/a
155	Yemen	0,492	0,492	-2	-0,002	+0,032
156	Afghanistan*	0,444	0,444	n/a	n/a	n/a

■ Eastern Europe and Central Asia ■ Middle East and North Africa ■ East Asia and the Pacific ■ Latin America and the Caribbean ■ North America ■ South Asia ■ Sub-Saharan Africa ■ Western Europe

* New countries in 2021

Notes

"–" indicates score or rank is unchanged from the previous year.

"n/a" indicates that the country was not covered in previous editions.

CHAPTER 7

Measuring income inequality – A holistic approach

7.1 INTRODUCTION

Income inequality across South Africa as a whole, as well as within organisations, has plagued the South African economy. Income inequality has traditionally been viewed from a single viewpoint, the Wage Gap, however the problem with making use of any isolated metric to quantify income inequality is that no single metric exists to encompass all aspects of income inequality. This chapter looks at multiple methods for identifying and addressing income inequality at both macro and micro-economic levels, and discusses the advantages and disadvantages of each approach. Furthermore, the overall benefits of using the discussed metrics in conjunction with one another in a multi-metric approach are explored. This provides the reader with a toolkit which can be used to analyse their remuneration policies and strategies from a holistic viewpoint rather than a single viewpoint. It allows the user to not only identify, but also address, income inequality at a more detailed level than has been done traditionally, and ultimately provides the user with a more effective means of addressing income inequality. We start with an overview of inequality.

7.1.1 *Overview of inequality*

Historically, the South African economy has been afflicted by income and wealth inequality, resulting from inequitable policies during the colonial and apartheid eras. When comparing every country's Gini Coefficient in terms of income and wealth, South Africa has persistently ranked in the top five most unequal countries in the world.

The Gini Coefficient measures inequality in income in a country or organisation – the higher the coefficient, the greater the inequality. A measure of 1 displays total inequality (where the highest earner earns all the pay), whilst a measure of zero shows no inequality (where all people earn exactly the same). This inequality has persisted in South Africa despite the first democratic elections having taken place in 1994 (see Figure 7.1 below).

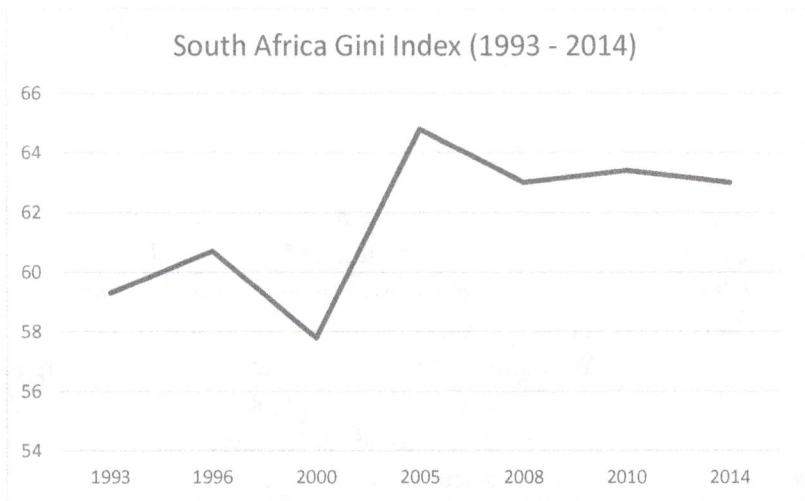

Figure 7.1: Historical view of South Africa's Gini Coefficient
*Source – World Bank Data: Gini Coefficient data is not published every year and all available data points between 1993 and 2014 have been used[60]

Figure 7.1 indicates that although there were initial gains in overall income equality at a macroeconomic level between 1993 and 2000, inequality increased significantly between 2000 and 2006, and is currently only slightly below the 2006 level. Currently, the 2005 figure of 0.64 is the highest reported by the World Bank for any country for which data is reported. In other words, according to the World Bank data, South Africa has the highest level of income inequality in the world.

It is very important to note that the national Gini Coefficient includes *ALL* individuals in the economy, both employed and unemployed. As South Africa has a very high unemployment rate, the overall Gini Coefficient is dramatically increased. If unemployment in South Africa was halved, the Gini Coefficient would come down to 0.48 (or 48), which is in line with the rest of the world. Halving CEO pay will not solve the problem.

Given these high levels of income inequality, it is not surprising that income inequality within individual companies has been the topic of much debate. The instrument most commonly used when measuring income inequality within a company is the Wage Gap, which can be defined as the ratio of the CEO's pay to the median worker's salary. Unfortunately, the element of pay used in this calculation is often not specified. This leaves this methodology open to interpretation, and hence abuse, as the person performing the calculation can decide on the element of pay to use (e.g. Total Guaranteed Package would return a lower ratio than Total Earnings). There are other limitations of using the Wage Gap as a measure of income inequality, which are discussed more robustly later in this chapter. The use of the Wage Gap in isolation can thus provide a distorted picture of the true state of inequality within an organisation.

The implementation of the Employment Equity Amendment Act 47 of 2013[61] has created a need for a more robust measure of internal equity that addresses company income inequality on a microeconomic rather than macroeconomic level within organisations. Macroeconomic studies have used a number of different methodologies for measuring income inequality at country or regional level. These methods include but are not limited to:

- Gini Coefficients

- Lorenz Curves

- Coefficients of Variation

- 10-10 Ratios

- Pay Differentials

- Palma Ratio

Each of these methodologies measure income inequality from a different perspective and provide the user with different information. If a methodology could be found which makes use of a number of different income inequality measures, the result would lead to a more robust understanding of the sources of income inequality within the organisation.

Although many countries in the world experience income inequality, South Africa is infamous for its own income inequality. This is discussed next.

7.2 INCOME INEQUALITY IN SOUTH AFRICA

Due to the effect of income inequality on the South African economy, a substantial number of policies have been created and implemented to curtail it. There is also a large amount of literature which addresses the concept of income inequality for South Africa as a whole, and within certain race, gender and education groups. Surprisingly, there is a shortage of research into inequality at an organisational or company level. The policy and research sections of this literature review will be reviewed separately, beginning with policy.

The Labour Relations Act 66 of 1995, as amended, and the Employment Equity Act 55 of 1998, as amended, were written to address systematic inequality. The Employment Equity Act makes provision for income differentials, where an employer must take measures to progressively reduce disproportionate income differentials (Employment Equity Act 55 of 1998, as amended – Chapter 3 Section 27).[62] This essentially places the onus on the employer to not only be aware of income inequality within their organisation, but to address it as well.

In an amendment to the Employment Equity Act, unfair discrimination is addressed by placing the onus of proof on the employer.[63] If there is a complaint of unfair discrimination within an organisation, the employer must prove why the alleged discrimination is not of an unfair nature. Section 6 specifically states that an employer cannot unfairly discriminate in terms of one or more of the following criteria: race; sex/ gender; pregnancy; marital status; family responsibility; ethnic or social origin; colour; sexual orientation; age; disability; religion; HIV status; conscience; belief; political opinion; culture; language; birth; or any arbitrary ground.

A new schedule to replace the previous schedule of maximum fines payable for contravening the Employment Equity Act has been included in the amendments to the Employment Equity Act.[64] This is an indication of government's increased commitment to addressing issues of unfair income inequality within the workforce. It should be noted that discrimination is not deemed to be unfair if it is in line with affirmative action or is inherent to the job. On 29 September 2014, the Draft Code of Good Practice on Equal Pay for Work of Equal Value was published.[65]

Work of equal value is defined within three categories:

- Same work: Work is identical or interchangeable.

- Substantially the same work: Work is not identical or interchangeable but sufficiently similar so that they can reasonably be considered to be the same. An objective assessment of actual duties and responsibilities required.

- Work of equal value: Different jobs but compare relative complexity, responsibility, decision-making level etc.

This requires a Job Evaluation system, as detailed in previous chapters.

As discussed, this legislation relates to unfair discrimination; discrimination of a fair nature is acceptable as long as there are acceptable reasons for the discrimination. Discrimination can be deemed to be fair if it is based on: seniority/length of service; qualifications/ability/competence/potential; performance/quality of work/quantity of work (provided that the performance evaluation system is equally applied); fixing a demoted employee's salary at a certain level until other employees in the same job category reach this level; temporary position for the purpose of training/gaining experience; shortage of relevant skill/market value in a particular job classification; any other relevant factor.

The legislation is not confined to remuneration, but also covers the terms and conditions of employment. In the context of this chapter, the discussion regarding inequality will be confined to remuneration only. As policy on income inequality has been communicated, the next section considers the research that has been conducted to provide further insight into the topic.

7.2.1   The impact on wage inequality

A significant amount of research has focused on the socioeconomic effects of income inequality. Specifically, this research has focused on the relationship between the distribution of income and health, as well as the relationship between the distribution of income and education. Mostafa, Saeed and Samira[66] found that larger levels of inequality in income distribution were negatively correlated with life expectancy and also had a negative effect on infant mortality rates. Figures 7.2 and 7.3 analyse the data using scatter plot diagrams and confirm these findings.

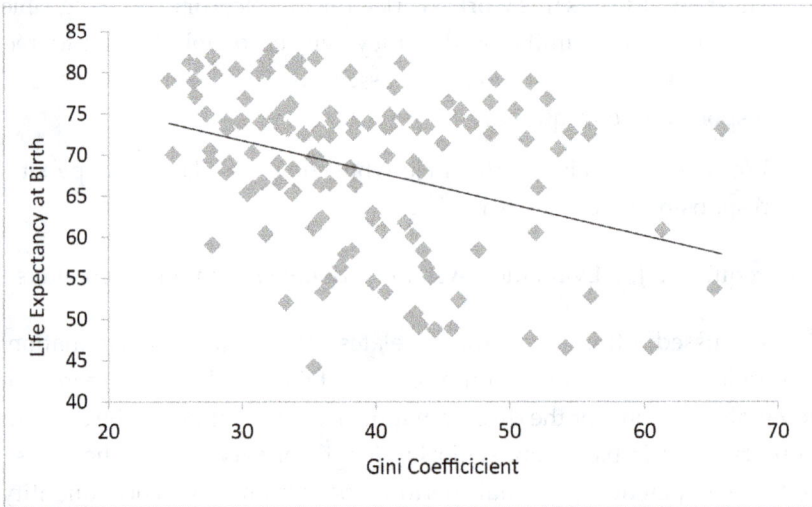

Figure 7.2: Correlation between income inequality and life expectancy at birth (Source: World Bank Data averaged between 2005 and 2014[67])

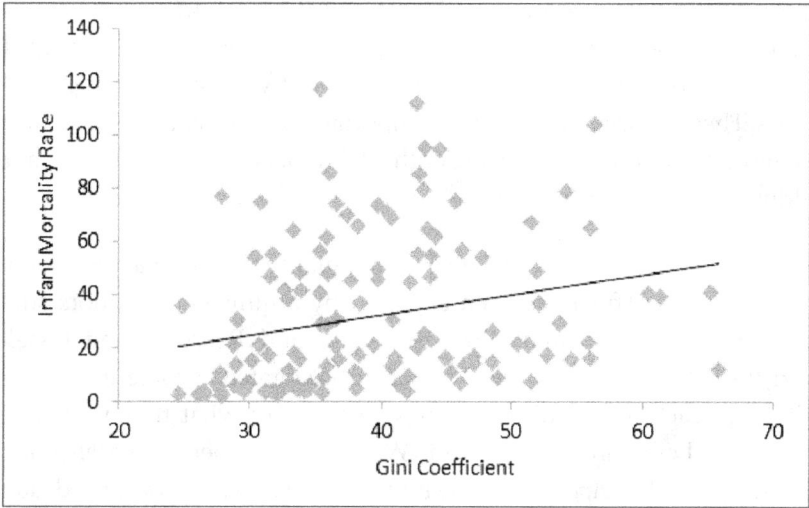

Figure 7.3: Correlation between income inequality and infant mortality rate per 1,000 live births (Source: World Bank Data averaged between 2005 and 2014[68])

De Gregorio and Lee found that there was a negative correlation between the distribution of income and average years of schooling.[69] They also found that increasing the average years of schooling leads to lower levels of income inequality.

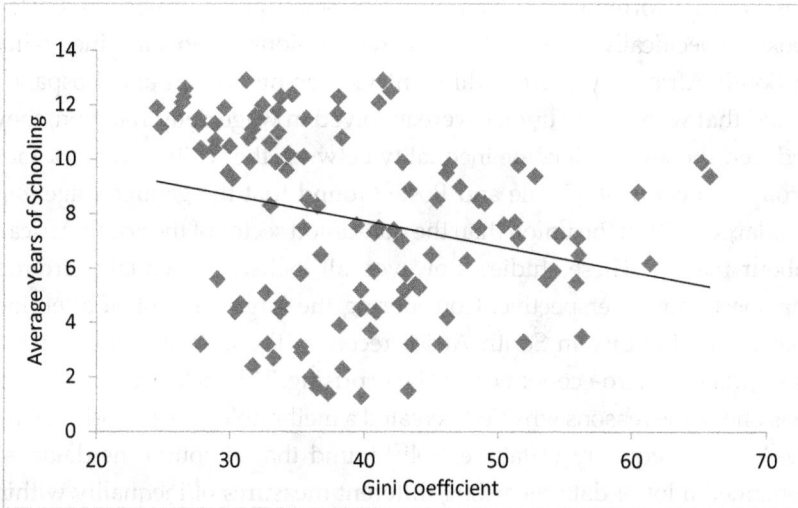

Figure 7.4: Correlation Between Income Inequality and Average Years of Schooling (Source: World Bank[70])

According to the sources used in Figures 7.2, 7.3 and 7.4, South Africa has a life expectancy at birth of 53.75 years, an infant mortality rate (per 1,000 live births) of 41.08, and an average number of years of schooling of 9.9 years. These figures emphasise the importance of reducing the inequality in the distribution of income in South Africa for social development, and ultimately economic, reasons.

Research into the subject of income inequality at the macroeconomic level in South Africa has been explored by a number of authors such as Leibbrandt, Finn and Woolard, Azam and Rospabe, and Casale and Posle.[71] All three of these papers investigated income inequality, although each took a different view in terms of what they wished to measure. Leibbrandt, Finn and Woolard's[72] paper, *Describing and Decomposing Post-Apartheid Income Inequality in South Africa*, used data from 1993 to 2008 to examine the overall changes in income inequality, as well as the inequality within and between different race groups. They concluded that overall, income inequality increased during this period due to a larger proportion of income being earned by the top earning income decile. When inequality was measured within and between race groups, they found that although it had declined between race groups, it had increased within each group.

Research performed by Azam and Rospabe[73] and Casale and Posle[74] looked specifically at the effects of trade unions on income inequality in South Africa, albeit from different viewpoints. Azam and Rospabe[75] found that when trade unions were involved in wage determination, they reduced the level of income inequality between the white and black race groups. In contrast, Casale and Posle[76] found that the gender wage gap was larger within the union than the non-union sector of the South African labour market. These studies, however, all looked at inequality from a macroeconomic perspective. Considering the large amount of attention that internal equity in South Africa receives, the lack of studies at the enterprise or micro-economic level is surprising. This lack of available data was one of the reasons why Solt[77] created a methodology for standardising the World Inequality Database. Solt[78] found that although the database contained a lot of data regarding different measures of inequality within individual countries, the methodologies followed were not consistent.

Helpman, Itskhoki and Redding[79] analysed the reasons behind Pay Differentials and income inequality within companies, finding that larger companies and companies that exported their products/services tended to pay higher wages. They also found that opening an economy from a previous state of autarchy resulted in an initial increase in income inequality and unemployment. As no noticeable trend was evident regarding what happens to income inequality and unemployment in the long run, it can be concluded that these initial transformations in the economy did not necessarily persist.

Chiu, Luk and Tang[80] made use of remuneration data from a number of companies in China in order to test for various levels of inequality. These tests were carried out by size, sector and education in order to see which sub-categories within these categories suffered from the highest levels of income inequality. In order to find the best way of measuring income inequality within companies in South Africa, it is essential to undertake this sort of micro-economic/company-based analysis.

If the sample is large enough, there are a number of measures of inequality in macroeconomics which could be applied to the micro-economic/company environment. The Lorenz Curve, developed by Max O. Lorenz in 1905, and the subsequent Gini Coefficient developed by Corrado Gini in 1912, are two examples of such measures. In order to fully understand the nature of inequality within an organisation and form a holistic view, a mix of both macroeconomic and micro-economic techniques are required.

The next section focuses on relevant methodologies and analyses related to income inequality.

7.3 METHODOLOGIES AND ANALYSES

This section will focus on methodologies and how each can be applied and interpreted.

The methodologies which will be evaluated are:

- Wage Gap
- 10-10 Ratio

- Palma Ratio

- Lorenz Curve and Gini Coefficient

- Coefficient of Variation

- Pay Differentials

7.3.1 *Wage gap*

The Wage Gap is one of the most commonly used measures of income inequality at the microeconomic (company) level. There have been a number of different methodologies used in order to calculate a 'Wage Gap', and as a result, the credibility of these figures reported in the media is often the subject of debate. The methodology used by the United States Securities Exchange Commission (SEC) is calculated as:

$$\frac{CEO\ Pay}{Median\ Pay\ of\ (Paterson\ Grade)\ A,B,C\ Band\ Employees}$$

This calculation provides the user with the ratio of how many times higher the CEO's pay (chosen element of pay) is than the median worker's pay. The median worker in this case is defined as the median A, B and C band worker and excludes management and specialist staff. The benefits of using this methodology are that it is simple to compute, easily understood and inclusive from the point of view of the staff (denominator of the equation), as the median of all Paterson A, B and C band workers is used.

The weakness of the Wage Gap methodology is that it is easily manipulated (e.g., by simply halving the CEO's pay, the ratio will halve even if there has been no gain to the worker's welfare, and the grade of the 'median employee' is unknown, therefore an organisation with a high number of lower level employees is more likely to have a higher wage gap (and vice versa).

The second limitation is related to the grade of the median employee who is being evaluated. A company with many lower graded positions and employees will have a lower median general staff grade than a company that is more technical and requires a higher level of skill to operate.

There are a number of measures of income inequality which can be calculated, all with their own benefits and limitations.

7.3.2   10-10 Ratio

In macroeconomics, the 10-10 Ratio (sometimes called a Rich/Poor or R/P Ratio) is often used as a crude measure of inequality when all the data needed to calculate a Gini Coefficient are not available. Although it is similar to the Wage Gap (in that it measures the ratio of the highest paid employee to the lowest paid employee), it is more inclusive as it uses a number of employees (rather than a single employee) as the numerator. It is calculated as:

$$\frac{\sum Highest\ 10\%\ of\ Employee's\ Pay}{\sum Lowest\ 10\%\ of\ Employee's\ Pay}$$

The benefits of this methodology are that it is easy to calculate; it is more inclusive than the standard Wage Gap in terms of how the numerator is calculated; it cannot be manipulated and if more data are available, it can quite easily be converted to a 20-20 ratio which would provide more information.

The disadvantages are that it does not provide information regarding the other 80% of the sample, and limited inference can be made as the distribution between the top and bottom 10% is unknown. The 10-10 Ratio is therefore best used in conjunction with a Wage Gap analysis, as it will alert the user to structural issues within the data if they return significantly different results. This method illustrates the need to make use of both the Wage Gap and the 10-10 Ratio when making decisions regarding income inequality between the top and bottom earners in a company. The Wage Gap (rather than the 10-10 Ratio) spotlights the CEO's pay, however the it can be easily manipulated by simply changing the CEO's pay. In contrast, at least 10% of employees need to have their pay altered in order to manipulate the 10-10 Ratio, making it more resistant to the possibility of being subject to game/tournament theory. As a result, the 10-10 Ratio is more inclusive when analysing employee welfare (in terms of pay) than the Wage Gap is.

7.3.3 *Palma Ratio*

In macroeconomics, the Palma Ratio is defined as the ratio of the richest 10% of the organisation's share of pay divided by the lowest 40%'s share. It is based on the work of Chilean economist Gabriel Palma, who found that middle class incomes almost always represent about half of gross national income, while the other half is split between the richest 10% and poorest 40%. Although it is similar to the 10-10 Ratio (in that it measures the ratio of the highest paid employees to the lowest paid employees), it is more inclusive than the 10-10 Ratio or Wage Gap as it uses a larger number of employees (rather than a single employee). It is calculated as:

$$(\sum [\text{Highest 10\% of Employee's Pay}]) / (\sum [\text{Lowest 40\% of Employee's Pay}])$$

7.3.4 *Lorenz Curve and Gini Coefficient*

The Lorenz Curve and Gini Coefficient are traditionally used in macroeconomics to measure the inequality within a distribution (in this case, income). The Lorenz Curve is a graphical illustration of the distribution of pay (from lowest to highest). The X-Axis is the number of individuals in the sample, ranked from the lowest to highest earning, while the Y-Axis is the cumulative income earned as a percentage of the total. In Figure 7.5, the first 10% of cumulative income is earned by approximately 20% to 25% of the sample. Similarly, the last 10% of cumulative income is earned by the highest earning 1% or 2%. Only the employed are considered in this chapter, therefore the term 'income' is tantamount to the individual's total guaranteed package.

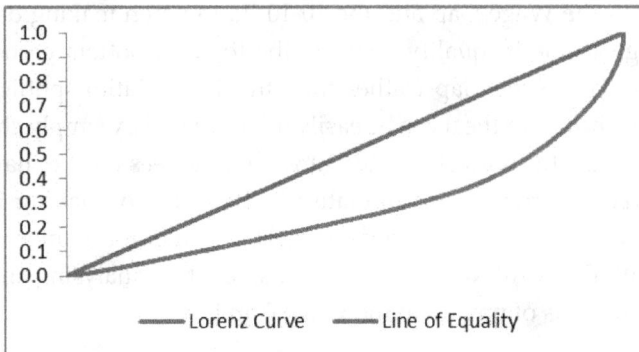

Figure 7.5: A Lorenz Curve

The Gini Coefficient is calculated from the Lorenz Curve. In layman's terms it measures the area between the 'Line of Equality' (when everyone earns exactly the same) and the Lorenz Curve, which is the cumulative distribution of all incomes in the sample, ranked from lowest to highest. The greater the distance (area) between the Line of Equality and the Lorenz Curve, the more unequal the income distribution is. The methodology can be simply stated as follows:

$$\frac{Area\ between\ Line\ of\ Equality\ \&\ Lorenz\ Curve}{Total\ Area\ Under\ Line\ of\ Equality}$$

The benefits of this methodology are that it makes use of the entire population of the sample rather than only a subsection, and therefore provides a more inclusive picture of income inequality. For over a century it has been recognised in economics as one of the leading measures of income inequality.

The weaknesses associated with this methodology are that a small sample may result in biased results, it can be computationally difficult to calculate, and it does not provide a measure of inequality within sub-sections of the population. The Gini Coefficient's ability to provide an all-inclusive measure of income inequality is the most advantageous feature of this methodology. A methodology which provides a measure of inequality between sub-sections is the Coefficient of Variation. It may seem counterintuitive that the Gini Coefficient for the whole of South Africa (not just the employed) exceeds the Gini Coefficient for each industry. The reason for this is that in this analysis, only employed persons are included. In contrast, South Africa's overall Gini Coefficient (reported by the World Bank) includes all persons in the economy, and as stated earlier, South Africa's high unemployment rate increases the overall Gini Coefficient.

7.3.5 Coefficient of Variation

In statistics, the Coefficient of Variation is defined as a normalised measure of dispersion within a sample. It is calculated as:

$$\frac{Sample\ Standard\ Deviation}{Sample\ Median}$$

This methodology allows one to analyse how dispersed an individual's pay is relative to the rest of their peer group (sample). In the case of measuring income inequality at the micro-economic/company level, the sample would include other employees at the same grade as the individual being assessed.

The benefits of this methodology are that it can be used to analyse sub-samples within a population (e.g., it can be used to calculate inequality within each grade), it can be used to measure macro and micro levels of inequality and therefore on its own it can provide more information than other measures, and it is easier to calculate than other methodologies, such as the Theil Index, which analyses inequality within sub-samples. The disadvantages of this methodology are that a large enough sample within each sub-sample is required in order to be able to make comparisons between sub-samples and draw significant inference from the analysis; biased results can be produced if the distribution of the data is far from a normal distribution, as the standard deviation may be excessively high due to outliers in the data set. However, given the weaknesses of this methodology it would not be prudent to simply use this method in isolation.

7.3.6 Pay Differentials

Pay Differentials are typically calculated in order to express one individual's pay as a ratio of another individual or sample median's pay:

$$\frac{Individual's\ Pay}{Other\ Individual\ or\ Sample\ Median\ Pay}$$

If the numerator is replaced by 'CEO Pay' and the sample median in the denominator was 'Median A, B and C Band Workers', this becomes the Wage Gap which we addressed earlier in this chapter. What separates this section from the section on the Wage Gap is ability of this methodology to be combined with the Coefficient of Variation in order to provide meaningful information regarding the concept of Equal Pay for Work of Equal Value. The Coefficient of Variation allows one to identify the grades which contain the largest amount of income inequality, while Pay Differentials allow one to identify the exact individuals who are causing the inequality at each extreme (low and high outliers). By addressing the sources of the income inequality within each grade, the income inequality within each grade will reduce, hence reducing the overall weighted average of the Coefficient of Variation. This ultimately results in lower levels of income inequality between workers who are performing substantially the same work and increased compliance with the Equal Pay for Work of Equal Value policy.

7.4 CONCLUSION

Income inequality has been at the forefront of many socioeconomic debates within South Africa and the rest of the world. Income inequality, at a macroeconomic level, is inherent to the South African economy as a result of the colonial and apartheid eras, which were in place for much of South Africa's modern history. This legacy of income inequality is not only at macroeconomic level but can often be found within organisations. This inequality has typically been measured using the Wage Gap.

The Wage Gap provides a good starting point for addressing income inequality within an organisation, but on its own does not provide a holistic view. The five measures of income inequality all have their own strengths and weaknesses, however the weaknesses can be mitigated by making use of multiple measures of income inequality. If a multi-measure approach is followed, the concept of income inequality can be addressed from a more holistic point of view than in isolation.

In the context of the Equal Pay for Work of Equal Value policy, a multi-measure approach allows for the identification of income inequality at various levels, namely, across the entire organisation, within individual grades, and at an individual level within grades or jobs. It is important to note that a year-on-year comparison within an organisation has much value, as it reflects improvement within a structure. A holistic and realistic view of income inequality within an organisation emerges when income inequality is addressed at each of the levels discussed previously in this chapter. This view will meet both policy and socioeconomic demands, and will ultimately translate into a more equitable labour market.

The next chapter outlines Job Evaluation in the new world of work. It contrasts the previous methods of Job Evaluation to the current and emerging methods, and brings light to the limitations of the past methods and the benefits of emerging methods.

CHAPTER 8

Job Evaluation in the new world of work

8.1 INTRODUCTION

As set out in detail previously, Job Evaluation is the systematic and objective process of comparing one job to another within an organisation to arrive at different job levels. Job evaluation can be a powerful tool in an organisation in terms of creating internal equity, as well as a base for measuring external equity, however it is a complex process. Anticipation of the pitfalls and potential of Job Evaluation can make a significant difference in an organisation.

To achieve organisational equity, a process and system has to be implemented across a wide range of business units or functions, so as to evaluate the relative complexity between positions. This can be a very time-consuming exercise. This is exacerbated when certified evaluators and validators are scattered across the country or, in some cases, internationally, or where there is a mix of home-based and office-based employees. It would be inconvenient and expensive to get all members of a Job Evaluation panel around the same table to evaluate and validate jobs in a company. Based on this, most organisations will require a Job Evaluation system that is accessible from anywhere – both nationally and internationally.

The new world of Job Evaluation involves less time-consuming meetings/methodologies/processes, as well as systems that offer a lot of flexibility that are technologically advanced, integrating and aligning Job Evaluation with other Human Resources processes and systems. The increasing demand from companies to implement web-based Job Evaluation systems, as well as less time-consuming processes to support these systems, has changed the new world of Job Evaluations. Based on this, there is an increasing demand from organisations to implement web-based Job Evaluation systems, i.e., systems that are accessible from anywhere. The next section will discuss the technological developments that have impacted Job Evaluation.

8.2 TECHNOLOGICAL DEVELOPMENTS IMPACT JOB EVALUATION

Technological developments have motivated companies to implement or adapt to new or modern Job Evaluation approaches, methodologies and systems. As companies grow from being owner-managed, more formal systems need to be implemented that 'explain' why employees earn what they do. Job evaluation and salary structures provide the cornerstone to this. During the process of Job Evaluation, we ask questions about the tasks being performed in a particular job, the relationship of jobs to each other, overlapping job content, and responsibilities. The content provided in the job descriptions can be effectively used for job design and job enrichment programmes. Job evaluation systems have to be flexible to accommodate the changing, dynamic environments within the market as well as in the organisation.

8.2.1 *Job evaluation systems – from manual to web-based*

Due to the new way of work that is increasingly performed online and remotely, Job Evaluations have shifted from manual methodologies to web-based methodologies. Manual job evaluation systems have several limitations, including the following factors: they are *cumbersome to maintain and update* as manual record keeping is required; they have limited *accessibility* (as you need to be present whilst doing the grading); *customisation* is limited as paper-based definitions are used and there is no customisation of factors/statements; *no integration* exists as they operate as a standalone system which cannot be integrated with other HR systems; they are *subjective* with no built-in validation criteria, therefore statements are open to interpretation and strong influencing/ manipulation by expert users who know the system; and *internal/external benchmarking against other similar jobs* has to be done manually, which is a very time consuming and costly process.

On the other hand, web-based systems have several advantages, including: they are *user friendly* as they are easy to use and maintain, and provide flexible and real-time reports; they have the advantage of *accessibility* as they can be accessed from anywhere (both nationally and internationally); *customisation* of factors/statements/questions of the system can be personalised for clients to meet their unique requirements; they have *endless integration possibilities* as they can integrate with online HR, job profiling, survey and recruitment systems; they are *objective* as they have built-in validation criteria to ensure valid end results (job grades) and consistency between panel members who sit at different locations; and they may be *regularly updated* so that there are job grade benchmarks to compare against.

8.2.2 *Formal panel meetings around the table to evaluating from your workstation or home*

Job evaluation discussions have changed from formal to more informal means, i.e., formal panel meetings in the office have been replaced with evaluations conducted in your own house or workstation. Formal panel meetings are accompanied by a number of limitations: they are *time consuming* (one person can only evaluate a maximum of six jobs per day); they are *costly* as senior and top management evaluate jobs and/or they are consultant-driven, and training is also expensive; they are *centralised*, meaning that members from other provinces need to be flown to other provinces/offices; they are *subjective*, in that statements are open for interpretation and strong influencing/manipulation by expert users who know the system; and they have a *lack of credibility* if they are only driven by HR and/or if there is no consistency in applying the definitions (lack of transparency). Despite their limitations, formal panel meetings also offer some advantages, as *line managers/jobholders/union/discipline experts* can be called in to provide more information should it be required.

In contrast, web-based evaluations from workstations or homes have the following advantages: there is *flexibility in time and location* since panel members can evaluate from anywhere in the world and at a time that is convenient to them; they are *decentralised*, allowing panel members to evaluate from different provinces/countries using online conference tools; *line managers/jobholders/union/discipline experts* can participate in the Job Evaluation process from their workstations without influencing other panel members and without seeing the job grade results or selections made by other panel members; they are *more objective* as panel members cannot be influenced (they evaluate separately from different locations and cannot view evaluation results or selections from other panel members); and they have *more credibility* as Job Evaluation results can be defended by using real-time and flexible job grade benchmark information and reports.

Having discussed the benefits related to the modern way of conducting Job Evaluations, the next section discusses what a modern Job Evaluation system is comprised of.

8.2.3 *Features of a successful, modern Job Evaluation system*

Successful, modern Job Evaluation systems have the following in common: they are *web-based, providing 24/7 access* to users across the world; they run on a *secure site* (https site with Thawte certificate, data encryption and password control); they have *flexible security settings* (functionality and administrator rights); they provide a *tracking history* for Job Evaluation sessions; they have a *management information system* – providing a database with all relevant information, job profiles, validated Job Evaluation results, job grade and salary benchmarks, comparison reports, additional notes, etc.; they have *flexible configurable processes and functionalities* with personalised factors, questions/statements and help screens; they have *translated factors, questions/statements and help screens for international organisations*; they *interface/integrate* with other *web-based HARM systems*; they provide *national/international and industry-specific benchmark jobs* that are updated on a regular basis; they *link to salary benchmarking information* that is updated on a regular basis; they provide *cross-correlations to other major Job Evaluation systems*; they are able to *integrate with a job profiling system* or provide a *fully integrated job profiling system*; they are *easy to use* as they are intuitive and user-friendly with *automatic workflow processes* on the system; they have *sophisticated built-in validation criteria* which highlights inconsistencies in Job Evaluation results and between Job Evaluation panel members; they have the *ability to add records of information* that are salient to a particular position and organisation; they are *real-time, flexible and have a wide variety of informative reports* that can be *exported to Excel, Word and Adobe Acrobat*, etc.; they provide a *suggestion box/online communication with users* so that clients can suggest changes/new developments; and they provide *online updates on enhanced functionalities or new developments*.

8.3 POPULAR MISCONCEPTIONS ON JOB EVALUATIONS

There are several misconceptions about Job Evaluations that need to be overcome, as these diminish the credibility of the Job Evaluation, limit buy-in from stakeholders of the process, and affect the functionality of the process. To ensure the success of the Job Evaluation process, the misconceptions that need to be rectified are listed below.

Organisational structures and job descriptions/profiles are not prerequisites for Job Evaluation

There is a direct correlation between the validity of job grades and the availability of clearly defined and approved organisational structures and job descriptions/profiles before Job Evaluation sessions. An organisational structure (indicating the job's positioning within the organisation) and job description/profile (indicating the job's responsibilities within the organisation) play a critical part in the validity of the job grade result. An organisational structure indicates the difference in the role of the manager's job and that of the job being evaluated, as well as the type of functions reporting into the job being evaluated.

The compiled job responsibilities must be clear amongst all parties concerned and must be ratified and in place before the evaluation of a job. Both the line manager and jobholders must sign the job descriptions/profiles to ensure that all parties involved have the same understanding of the responsibilities allocated to the job. Based on these documents, the Job Evaluation panel members can prepare for the Job Evaluation interviews and not pose irrelevant questions to the jobholder. Due to this, the time of the Job Evaluation session will be shortened and the involved parties will have more credibility in the end result based on the informed questions asked during the interview session. In short, no Job Evaluation sessions should take place unless the job, job content and the role thereof within the hierarchical level and structure has been investigated and clarified properly.

Job evaluation evaluates the person and not the job

Job evaluation panel members can fall into temptation when evaluating jobs by referring to the current jobholder, as they could be new to the job and therefore not fulfil all the tasks expected from the job, which will result in the under-evaluation of the job or the jobholder based on his/her current level of competence. The individual in the job could also be performing tasks not normally expected of the job, resulting in an over-evaluation of the job. It is therefore important that the work content and responsibilities are evaluated without reference to the performance or abilities of the current or future jobholder. The assumption is made that the jobholder can already perform the job according to the average standards and requirements of the job. **The golden rule is to always evaluate a job as if it is newly created with no current jobholders.**

Job evaluation takes volume of work into account

Workload or work volume is about the quantity of similar tasks performed in the execution of the job. Volume does not affect job complexity, i.e., more of the same tasks do not make a job more complex.

Job evaluation takes abnormal circumstances into account

Ignore unlikely or rare events and once-off situations and rather concentrate on the key performance areas of the job. Apply the '60/40' or "Is it a critical, ongoing part of the job?" rule consistently across all the Job Evaluation sessions to ensure that only responsibilities that form a regular part of the job are taken into account.

Job evaluation takes market factors into account

Factors such as scarcity of skills, non-performance, power and politics, etc. do not form part of the job content or responsibilities. These are remuneration issues and should only be taken into account during the structuring of the individual's pay.

Job evaluation takes future situations/possibilities into account

Evaluate the job content and responsibilities according to the mode of operation in the present time, without reference to any functions that used to be part of the job or could possibly be added in the future or any changes that might happen at a much later stage. By doing this, the Job Evaluation panel members avoid the risk of over evaluating the job if these additional tasks do not materialise in the future. Once those aspects are in place, the job can be re-evaluated.

Job evaluation can be used as a tool to keep employees from resigning

Job evaluation should not be used as a tool to retain certain people because of their skills or as an effort to keep them from resigning – the remuneration strategy should be used to address this.

There is no need for a validation panel to verify Job Evaluation results

The main objective of validation panel is to verify evaluated job grade results to ensure fairness, integrity, consistency and alignment across the organisation. The validity of these verified results are often questioned within organisations based on the feeling that the stronger members of the panel can influence the rest of the panel members to 'swing' the results. To overcome these possible influences, software has been developed to assist validation panel members to review and verify job grade results at a time and place convenient to them and on their own. Successful validation functions should provide information on: 1) industry-specific position benchmarks (to ensure industry market equity); 2) national position benchmarks (to ensure national market equity); and 3) internal position benchmarks (to ensure internal equity).

An employee cannot appeal against the Job Evaluation result or process

Employees can most definitely appeal against unfair Job Evaluation results or processes. Under normal circumstances, appeals relating to or dissent about the Job Evaluation and validation process can be categorised as being:

- *Technical*, i.e., related to the technical or other content of the Job Evaluation system; or

- *Process*, i.e., related to the manner in which processes and procedures used in Job Evaluation and validation were or were not applied.

All appeals should be put in writing and referred to the HR department. Should satisfaction not be obtained in this way, the HR department will refer it to the Chairperson of the validation panel. The most independent way to settle the manner would be to refer it to an external remuneration specialist, who will validate the job grade result.

Job evaluation sessions are time consuming and costly

Since a Job Evaluation/validation panel usually consists of fairly high-level employees in an organisation, the financial implications in terms of hours "lost" during such a process is a major concern to most organisations.

Job evaluation software that is web-based ensures that these time consuming Job Evaluation sessions can be conducted from anywhere in the world and at a time (even after hours) convenient to the facilitators and/or validators, thus minimising the time required for the process.

Job evaluation systems are inflexible

Organisations need a customised system to evaluate their multi-disciplined (operational, production, marketing, sales, advertising, financial, etc.) and professional (legal, scientific, research, pharmacology, information technology, medical, etc.) jobs. Job evaluation systems with industry-specific and environmental analysis questions are now available; customisation of the terminology in web-based versions can easily be updated; and changes can be reflected immediately to users anywhere in the world.

Job evaluation systems are difficult to maintain

Job evaluation systems have to be enhanced and updated on a regular basis to ensure they keep abreast of changes in the organisation. On a web-based system all the evaluated jobs are automatically stored on one database, and are available at all times and accessible from anywhere in the world, with no need for integration of data. Any changes to these web-based systems will be reflected immediately in real time.

Job evaluation processes have developed recently in quantum leaps. Electronic systems are now customisable, easy to use, easy to access, and reduce the effect of the most common misconceptions surrounding the subject.

8.4 FLEXIBILITY OF THE JOB EVALUATION SYSTEM

The Job Evaluation system must be flexible and grow with the organisation's needs. If it is perceived to be a dynamic, living system, it can even become a motivational influence. There should be procedures in place for updating job descriptions and subsequent re-evaluation. It is this flexibility that is at the heart of Job Evaluation in the new world of work.

8.4.1 Working in teams

If the organisation moves towards teams, these teams need to form part of Job Evaluation so that salary benchmarking can be done. One way of addressing a team grade is to broad-band the jobs that form part of the team into one broad band. Figure 8.1 shows diagrammatically how teamwork and flexibility put pressure on a traditional graded structure (almost "demanding" the implementation of broad-banding).

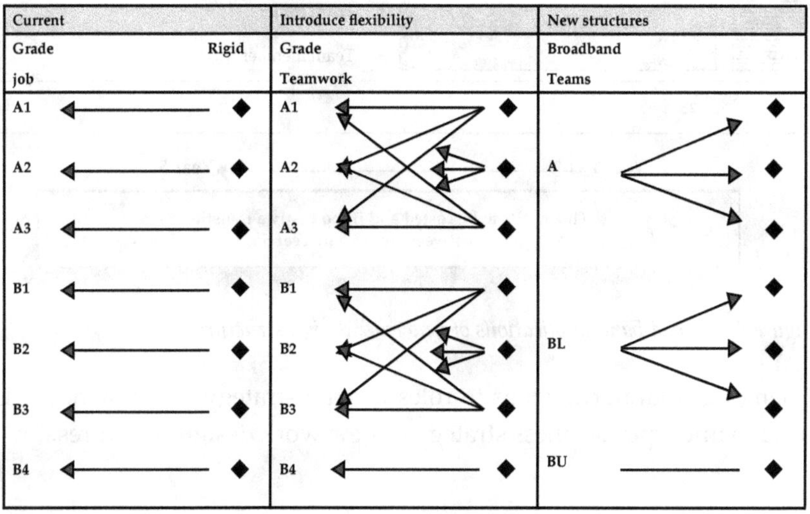

Figure 8.1: Effect of teamwork and job flexibility on broad-banding

8.4.2 *Increase in responsibility from job to role*

The second scenario of flexibility is where a job was tightly described and boxed in, but is now much more flexible where the employee needs to understand and work up and down the value chain. Employers then tend to write a broader role description. Role descriptions can span several jobs, for example, the job description of debtors clerk, creditors clerk and filing clerk are combined into a role description of finance clerk. The Job Evaluation system needs to be flexible enough to accommodate this. Usually, the most complex task performed is graded, which puts it at the higher grade. This can be expensive and a good alternative is to create pay progression milestones within the broad-band so that as skills are acquired, the employer is paying for them. An example of this can be seen in Figure 8.2 below, where three jobs in the mining industry became one role.

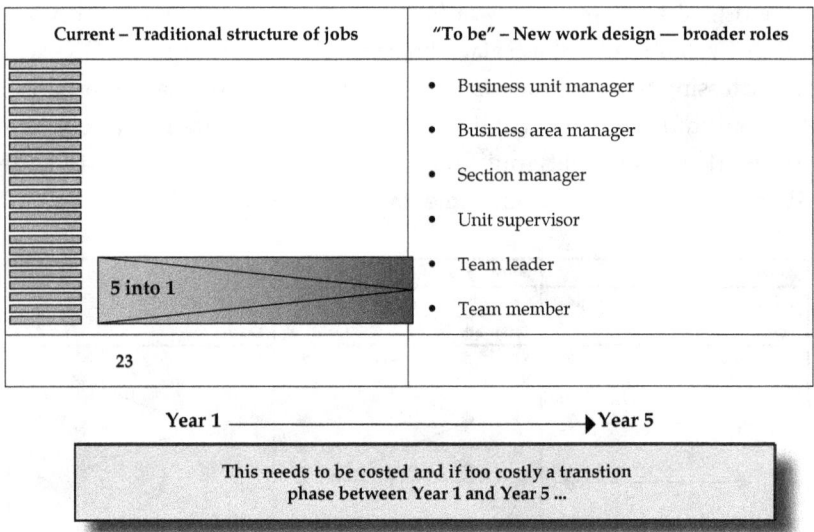

Current – Traditional structure of jobs	"To be" – New work design — broader roles
5 into 1	• Business unit manager • Business area manager • Section manager • Unit supervisor • Team leader • Team member
23	

Year 1 ————————————————→ Year 5

This needs to be costed and if too costly a transtion phase between Year 1 and Year 5 ...

Figure 8.2: Broad-band implications of new work design structure

Changing from narrow jobs to roles is not a strategy on its own, but is used to underpin business strategy or new work design structures.

8.4.3   *Work from anywhere (WFA)*

In this scenario where employees can choose to work from anywhere, the employer needs to change the job description from a list of activities to outputs and outcomes. Better still, is to also include the impact of the outcome. The Job Evaluation system needs to be flexible enough to accommodate grading outcomes and impact. The implication here is that the Job Evaluation system needs to have the compensable factors in it that can size the complexity of the outcome.

8.4.4   *Contingent workers*

The rise of the gig economy is also fuelling the growth of the contingent workforce. The first thing that comes to mind when thinking of a contingent workforce is the word 'contractor'. These workers contract to do a specific piece of work and then leave. It could take a week, a month, a year or several years depending on the size of the project. Many organisations still grapple with pricing the value of contract work, but the solution lies in the flexible Job Evaluation system, where the terms of reference or service level agreement with the contractor is graded and priced as though an employee was going to do it. It is then also easy to see if it is more cost effective to hire a full-time employee or not. Typically, contractors earn a small premium of around 25% relative to a full-time employee because the company does not need to pick up the costs of any benefits and the contractor has the risk of the contract being terminated at short notice.

8.5   IMPACT ON REMUNERATION STRUCTURES

Compared to a conventional salary structure, broad-band structures designed to accommodate teams, agile work, roles and WFA have fewer salary bands and broader minimum to maximum spreads. Broad-bands feature a few, relatively wide, pay ranges that retain many characteristics found in conventional salary administration processes. This is shown diagrammatically in Figure 8.3.

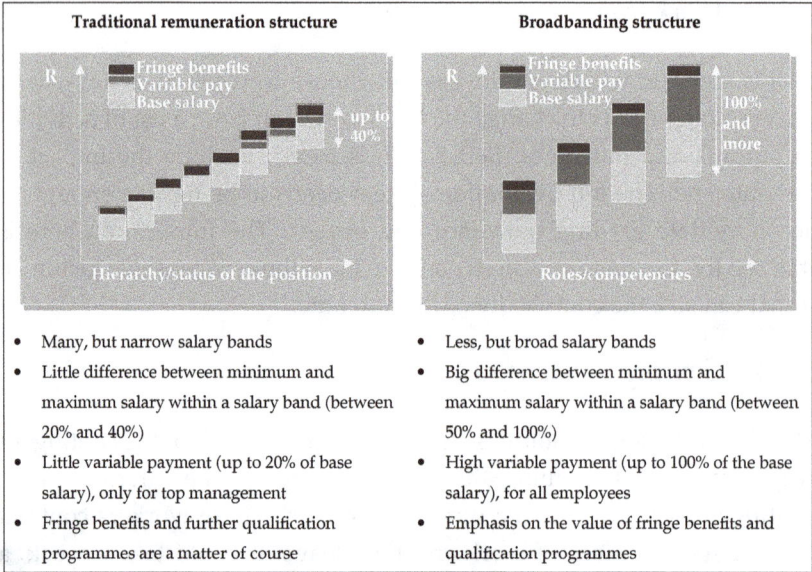

Traditional remuneration structure	Broadbanding structure
• Many, but narrow salary bands	• Less, but broad salary bands
• Little difference between minimum and maximum salary within a salary band (between 20% and 40%)	• Big difference between minimum and maximum salary within a salary band (between 50% and 100%)
• Little variable payment (up to 20% of base salary), only for top management	• High variable payment (up to 100% of the base salary), for all employees
• Fringe benefits and further qualification programmes are a matter of course	• Emphasis on the value of fringe benefits and qualification programmes

Figure 8.3: Traditional versus broad-band structure

Table 8.1 sets out some of the differences between typical traditional graded structures and typical broad-band structures.

Table 8.1: Comparison of traditional versus broad-band structures

Aspect	Traditional graded structures	Broad-band structures
1. Number of levels	15 to 26	6 to 12
2. Pay scale width (minimum to maximum for a grade or band)	30% to 100%	50% to 300%
3. Pay overlap between grades or bands	10% to 30%	20% to 40%
4. Career development	Moving up grades	Typically horizontal (bigger projects, stores, lines, shafts, cases, and so on)
5. Typical main focus	Job grading	Competence and performance

Aspect	Traditional graded structures	Broad-band structures
6. Pay delivery	Job grade, competence and performance Focus on job	Mostly competence and performance or both focus on person
7. System mostly controlled by	HR function	Line management
8. Market data	By grade is typically adequate unless position is scarce demanding a premium	By position or job family becomes necessary
9 Band descriptions	By grade or specific job title	By roles or level of work (Stratified Systems Theory – SST)
10. Job evaluation	In forefront and important	In the background as an administrative tool
11. Cost control	By policing	By empowerment

8.5.1 Remuneration and broad-bands

Movement through the broad-band, for example, from primary to operational to advanced operational, is usually dictated by the particular grading rules being used. An example would be broad-band Paterson grading rules. Movement within the pay scale of a broad-band level is usually dictated by the Pay Progression Policy (PPP). The most commonly used criteria for the PPP for individuals are:

- performance;
- track record and experience;
- market scarcity; and
- type of work.

8.5.2 Job family design

Broad-banding is often supported by the introduction of job family design, which helps with 'pegs' within broad pay scales. A job family is a series of jobs that are involved in work of the same nature but require different levels of skill, responsibility and competencies for each job level. The term 'job family' describes the key factors which differentiate one level from the next. For example, a personal assistant or secretarial job family may look as in Table 8.2:

Table 8.2: Example of a personal assistant or secretarial job family

Level	Job	Responsibility
4	Personal assistant to Chief Executive	Responsible for performing secretarial duties for the Chief Executive of a confidential nature, often liaising with key and/or important stakeholders.
3	Executive secretary	Responsible for performing secretarial duties for one or more Executive managers.
2	Senior secretary	Responsible for performing secretarial duties for one or more senior managers.
1	Junior secretary	Responsible for performing secretarial duties for one or more managers.

An entry-level junior secretary would be one who has recently graduated from school, who has little experience, whose skills are being developed, and who would be given responsibilities at a lower level than compared to, say, a senior secretary who has greater relevant job experience. On the other hand, a personal assistant would be someone with many years of experience, whose skills and competencies are exemplary and who completes the job duties of a high-level assistant. The 'value' of a position within this job family would therefore vary widely based on the individual's experience, competencies, and level of responsibility.

A pictorial example of an engineering job family showing the split or dual career path between the technical track and manager track is shown in Figure 8.4.

	PATERSON BAND	DESCRIPTOR
	F	Top management
	EU	General management
	EL	Senior management/ specialist
	DU	Middle management/senior professional
	DL	Management/ professional
	CU	Supervisory/ advanced operational
	CL	Technical/ operational
	BU	Administrators/ operational
	BL	Clerical
	A	Basic skills

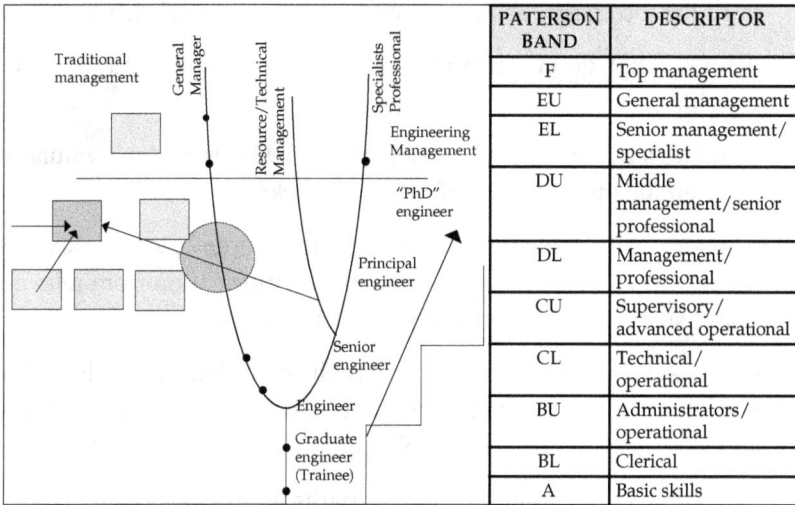

Figure 8.4: Engineering dual career path

8.5.3 Defining levels within a job family

Defining levels within a job family includes:

- Determining the advantages and disadvantages of a job family approach for your organisation and the benefits, if implemented, to the organisation.

- Determining the number of job families required, which is typically between five and ten.

- Describing the nature of work to be undertaken in each job family.

- Establishing the different levels of work in each family based on Job Evaluation, or alternatively, each level can be defined in terms of the accountability and competencies required to carry out work at this level.

8.5.4 Reasons for implementing a job families approach

There are several reasons for implementing a job families approach, i.e., it:

- supports de-layered, flatter structures, thereby reducing the need for structured Job Evaluation;

- provides job clarity, as accountabilities of roles are clearly defined;

- defines what good performance looks like in all of these work activities;

- provides a transparent and straightforward basis for Job Evaluation through the identification of levels of work;

- provides a straightforward link to the external pay market (job family structures are market-driven, and information from relevant salary surveys will need to be collated);

- outlines succession and career path planning (provides clear definitions for career paths within job families, across job families, and even diagonally to other job families); and

- provides clear definitions of career paths within jobs.

Employees in a job family are also empowered, because promotions focus on individual performance, development and training, based on the competencies required for each level of work.

8.5.5   Implications of this approach

The job family approach:

- improves competencies of the workforce through better selection and placement;

- increases training and development participation;

- increases retention of competent employees;

- improves individual performance and contribution;

- provides flexibility to line managers in staffing decisions;

- provides flexibility to line managers when assigning job duties; and

- may make salary management functional or job family-specific.

The Job Evaluation system and how it is applied has a direct knock-on effect on the remuneration structures. The internal teams looking after these need to work closely with each other and understand the impact of one on the other.

8.6 CONCLUSION

The future of Job Evaluation is flexible and technologically advanced, with less time-consuming meetings/methodologies/processes. Job evaluation will continue to evolve in an increasingly modern and flexible format. The focus will be on integrating and aligning Job Evaluation with other Human Resources processes and systems, based on a common conceptual competency base.

With the advancements in web-based video conferencing, the combination of web-based Job Evaluation will render 'same venue' Job Evaluation meetings obsolete in the future. Job evaluation is the systematic and objective process of comparing one job to another within an organisation to arrive at different job levels. It does so without looking at individual characteristics, personality or performance. All Job Evaluation systems do the same thing, i.e., rank jobs according to complexity of work. Job evaluation systems assist with equal pay for work of equal value considerations. Many organisations have started to outsource the grading of their job descriptions to keep it professional and impartial. Job evaluation fails when jobs are upgraded without a corresponding change of job content. Job evaluation systems need to be maintained and audits should be done every few years to secure the integrity of the system. Make sure that all the leaders have a good understanding of the system you have chosen. Considering the transformation of Job Evaluation, the next chapter, Chapter 9, focuses on the effect this change has had on the psychological contract.

CHAPTER 9

The psychological impact of the new way of Job Evaluation

9.1 INTRODUCTION

People tend to equate personal value and worth to the Job Evaluation grade allocated to their position. It is considered a reflection of their relative worth to the organisation and often the only means to determine the remuneration level of the job. Therefore, changes to the way in which jobs are designed and subsequently evaluated could have a major psychological impact on employees. This chapter focuses on job analysis and the actual job description, as well as job enrichment, which could contribute to employee engagement and overall well-being. The impact of these changes on the psychological contract is also deliberated upon.

9.2 THE TRADITIONAL APPROACH TO JOB ANALYSIS

Job analysis and the job description form the basis of most of the human resources activities.[81] Job analysis, the starting point for the development of the job profile or description, is typically described as a process of collecting information about a position by means of job analysis questionnaires, interviews or job observation. Firth mentioned that job descriptions, although important for a range of human resources activities, are usually outdated.[82] In addition, line managers often view job descriptions as a hassle due to the amount of time required to participate in such exercises. This process is required to eventually proceed to the evaluation process of the completed job description. Singh indicated that job analysis was already implied as far back as Socrates's concern about the nature of work in the 5th century BC, Diderot's report of job analysis activities and the nature and context of certain jobs in the trades, arts, and crafts in 1747, and Frederick Taylor's reference to job analysis as "the first of the four principles of scientific management" in 1916.[83] The first historical records of job analyses can be traced back to 1922, and already then the impact of structure and power were recognised in the description of jobs. Wilson referred to the drivers for job analysis processes as the legal, economic, organisational and technological context.[84]

Our deliberations on future job analysis practices are based on Wilson's report of several lessons learnt based on the history of job analysis practices over the past 100 years.[85] Firstly, there is the need to change the term *job analysis* itself, as it indicates inflexible approaches to job design. We recommend that this process be referred to as *job re-modelling*, based on company strategy, structure, environmental and contextual demands, as well as required outputs. This could relate to Siddique's description of the competency-focused job analysis approach where, for example, motivation, adaptability and teamwork orientation are emphasised as necessary for successful job performance.[86] Similarly, Oldham and Hackman proposed that the social interaction in a job be of the utmost importance for future considerations.[87] This differs from the standard or conventional job analysis approaches, where the emphasis is on basic job-related data such as responsibilities, knowledge, skills, a job specification and standard HR practices.

Secondly, we should ask ourselves which *purpose* should be ascribed to job analysis. Our recommendation is a *next assignment approach* rather than a fixed list of duties to ensure a more strategic approach. This is important not only in order to accommodate for agility and new or next normalities, but also to allow for a degree of flexibility. Oldham and Hackman highlighted that new work arrangements, for example virtual teamwork and flexibility arrangements, have put job design under constant pressure.[88] It still remains important to conduct regular job analyses or renewal exercises to ensure that the company's strategic direction is accommodated for, as "individuals do alter their roles in ways that are consistent with their skills and abilities".[89]

Thirdly, as job analysis could be costly from a time and monetary point of view, the application of Artificial Intelligence (AI) and/or drone technologies in, for example, conducting interviews or for observation purposes, could greatly reduce costs.

The fourth lesson learnt is that the way in which we *define* work is important. What would be the impact of the gig economy, new work arrangements and the impact on the psychological contract (those reciprocal expectations that both the employer and employee have of each other)? Most jobs can be considered to be in a state of flux, as there are "fundamental changes in the relationships among people, the work they do, and the organisations for which they do it".[90]

Thus, after considering the traditional approach to job analysis, we will now look at the future of job analysis and the predicted form that Job Evaluation is expected to take.

9.3 FUTURE OF JOB ANALYSIS

Scholars describe job analysis as "a strategic HR management practice with a significant impact on company performance" and as a way of gaining competitive advantage.[91] It must be acknowledged that collecting information to provide a comprehensive overview of creative, knowledge-intensive and managerial jobs has always been challenging. This will only become more challenging, as jobs change more frequently and new ways of work (telecommuting, job share, flexible working hours, working from home permanently and virtual teaming) continuously create different and novel job features.

The question should be asked how we can re-look at the job specification to state job-related requirements. Future genuine occupational qualifications will be extended to include preferred brain patterns, thinking styles, and the cognitive and emotional flexibility required for business sustainability.

Future job analysis methods will evolve into wearable electronics to track activities and possibly preferred brain patterns. AI will replace job interviewing and the format of reporting, that is, writing a job description or profile, will be communicated on a smartphone with reminders for deadlines etc. Irrespective of the approach that organisations follow, job design must be affected such as to procure the right talent so that strategic performance standards can be achieved.[92] Having examined the future of job analysis, the next section sheds light on the current role of the job description/profile.

9.4   THE ROLE OF THE JOB DESCRIPTION/ PROFILE

The cornerstone of most Job Evaluation systems is a well-defined job description/profile and a job specification. Usually, a job title carries and conveys the status and position of the job internally and externally to, for example, customers. It carries great psychological power, especially with regard to identifying the job in the structure. There is no denying that the position a person fills and the accompanying status could be highly motivational, impacting job satisfaction and individual performance. Equally as important as the job description is job design, which will now be discussed.

9.5   JOB DESIGN

Robbins and Judge described job design as "the way the elements in a job are organised".[93] Individual, organisational, technological and environmental factors greatly impact the design and redesign of jobs and motivation.[94] Mello noted that, "The greater the volatility in an organisation's environment, the greater the need for more flexible, adaptive work system".[95] In addition, the impact of technology on work and job design has been identified as the automation of repetitive jobs, more collaboration (teamwork) as hierarchies become flatter, as well as the creation of new routines and habits. In this regard, Mello emphasised less technically defined roles and broader, more flexible roles structured around strategic requirements.[96]

The challenge remains how we could design jobs to provide and extend career growth to knowledge workers and managers alike. Kalleberg cautioned against either institutional or structural mismatches, as this relates to individual skills, abilities, preferences and remuneration and the intended job.[97]

Job design usually applies job enrichment (vertical job enlargement or, in some instances, job rotation/loading). For the purposes of this chapter, the focus will be on job enrichment. Hackman and Oldham's job characteristic model on job design could still apply, but to ensure meaningful work, the scale must change (Figure 2.1).[98]

core job dimensions	→	critical psychological states	→	personal and work outcomes
role flexibility skill variety task identity	→	experienced sens-making experienced meaningfulness		life and job satisfaction high internal work motivation
innovation space	→	experienced self-efficacy		psychological safety
autonomy and job interdependence	→	experienced responsibility for outcomes of the work		high quality work performance
human/machine interaction (AI)	→	experienced sense of curiosity and achievement		high quality and sufficiency outputs low absenteeism and turnover (retention)
feedback and social support	→	knowledge of the actual results of the work activities		

↑   ↑   ↑

employee growth needs strength

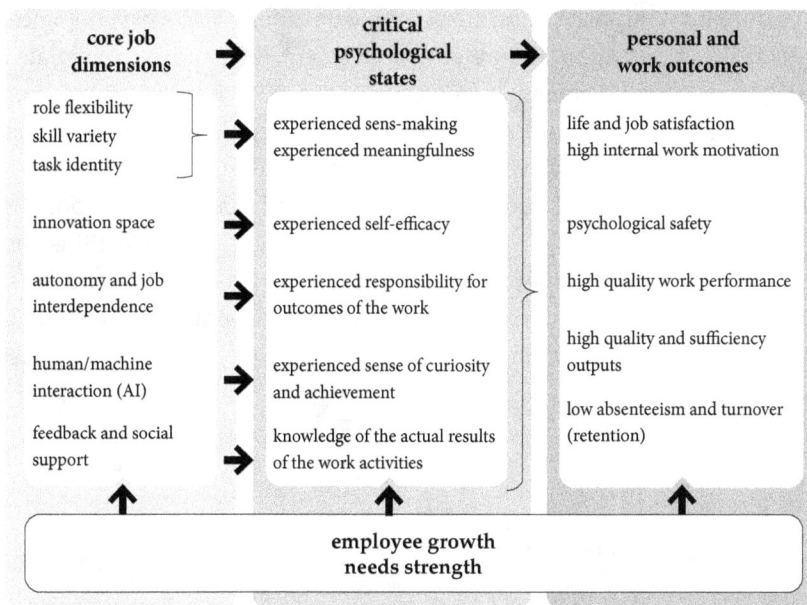

Figure 9.1: Job design model (adjusted from Hackman & Oldman and Morgenson & Humphrey[99, 100])

The core job dimensions as identified still apply by role. Flexibility was added to the core job dimensions of skill variety, task identity and task significance. Innovation space was coupled with autonomy to contribute towards the experience of responsibility for work outcomes. The identified critical psychological states resulting from the core job dimensions remain as is, while experienced sense-making and experienced self-efficacy have been added. To experience sense-making is important for the job incumbent, as anxiety coupled with too much role flexibility will increase. Experienced sense-making and subsequent experienced feelings of self-efficiency are critical psychological states for work motivation, satisfaction, quality performance and retention of talent. As Maddux emphasised, "self-efficacy is covered with human potential and possibilities, not limitations" and increases feelings of psychological well-being; it could be even more important for a person's success than actual abilities.[101]

With regard to personal and work outcomes, high internal work motivation, high quality work performance, high work satisfaction, low absenteeism and turnover will remain important for business sustainability. Important additions for the next normal are psychological safety, life satisfaction and retention of talent. It could be postulated that, as work arrangements change to settings such as working from home, absenteeism could fall away. Turnover could also become less prominent, with attention shifting to the retention of talent instead. Our alternative model for job design is based on a basic model of organisational behaviour by Robbins and Judge[102] as well as Mullins and McClean.[103] Job design thereby focuses on inputs, processes and outputs, at the individual, group, organisational and environmental levels. This approach is presented in Figure 9.2.

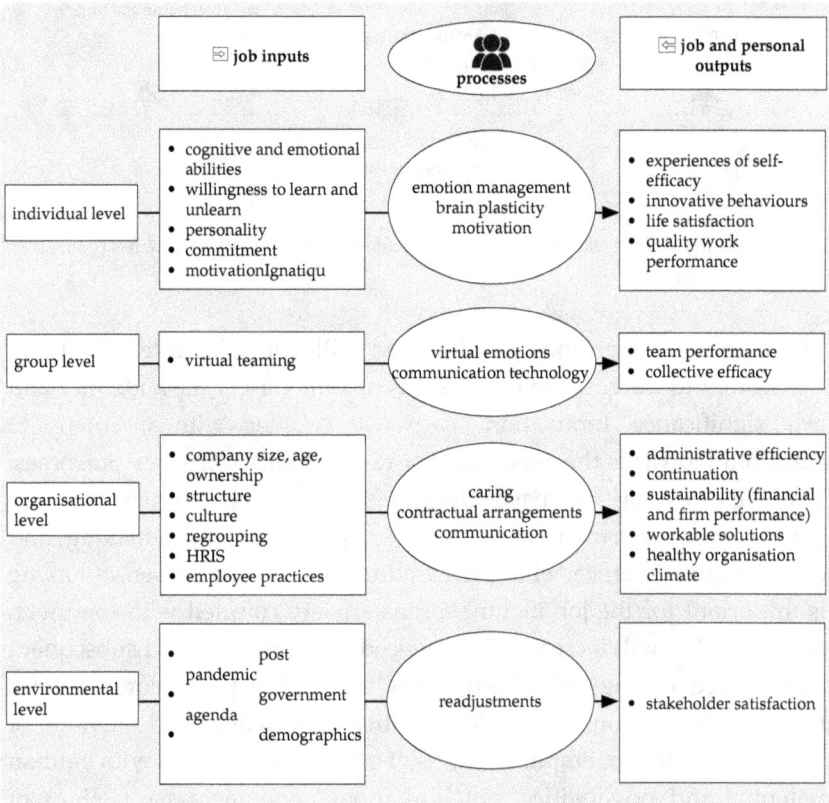

Figure 9.2: IPO model for job design (adjusted from Moerdyk et al.; Singh; Robbins & Judge[104, 105, 106])

The adjusted motivating potential score (MPS) developed by Hackman and Oldham[107] is shown in Figure 9.3. below. This index should provide an indication of role flexibility, skill variety, task identity, task significance and innovation space. As per the original MPS, the average will give an indication of experienced sense-making and meaningfulness for the individual in relation to the work performed. As explained by Mullins and McClean, these indicators are additive: the absence of one could to some extent be balanced by another. Autonomy, human/machine interaction and feedback are multipliers, which means that if any one of these is absent, the MPS will be zero and the "job would offer no potential to motivate the person".[108]

$$MPS = \frac{\text{job complexity} + \text{role flexibility} + \text{skill variety}}{+6} \times \text{autonomy} \times \begin{array}{c}\text{human/}\\\text{machine}\\\text{interaction}\end{array} \times \text{feedback}$$

task identity + task significance

Figure 9.3: Motivating Potential Score (MPS)

9.6 CONCLUSION

New forms of job design and analysis will impact the psychological contract and ultimate job engagement of knowledge workers and front-line staff. The contextual requirements will impact employees' fitness for the job, especially with regard to individual perceptions based on preferences, personality and required skills.[109] Human resources must empower employees to "accept the muddle", as "high performance is elusive and sometimes illusionary".[110] The disrupted energy flows have an impact on staff's psychological health, and clear answers as to how to address this in times of increasing uncertainty will remain one of the biggest challenges. This poses a risk to organisational sustainability in the form of disengagement, psychological wellness and overall health of employees.[111] Schwab and Davis have recommended policies and exemplary leadership behaviours that could help create more purposeful and socially conscious organisations.[112] Emotionalising organisations will provide fresh insights into job satisfaction and motivation[113], rethinking the people-organisation relationship.[114]

We would recommend that HR practitioners reconsider *job crafting*, whereby employees are more involved in customising, modifying and crafting their own jobs, or are at least consulted about the restructuring of their jobs. Through this, one could achieve an improved match between job demands and the available needs and skills of individual employees.[115]

The next chapter commences with suggestions of the way forward. It serves as a guide for organisations to address their HR practices to gear up for the expected trends so they may keep afloat in the 4IR.

CHAPTER 10

What should we do right now?

10.1 INTRODUCTION

Although the DNA of organisations is currently changing because of the 4IR and Covid-19, people are still achieving goals. There is no success formula for what should be done right now, and the "trouble is that in uncertain times, formulae for success are more attractive than ever before".[116] Even the current positive approach in human resources management must make room for a more deficit-based approach. As Kwon and Park pointed out, this is brought about by "employees [who] may lack sufficient internal motivation to change but are forced to participate in change nonetheless".[117] They also highlight that during such a deficit, the approach to organisational goal achievement is negatively impacted by the psychological distress experienced by employees.

In this chapter, different human resources conversations are proposed for consideration. HR directors are also cautioned that current decisions, although under different circumstances, will create precedents for the future. However, the current conditions preclude neither fairness and transparency, nor integrity and compassion.

Conversation 1: Employability and empowerment

New realities highlight employability skills as being extreme flexibility, discipline, learning and unlearning at a staggering pace, and an increased focus on soft skills. Remote teamwork and working from home require more dependability and emotion management from employees. These are coupled with shifting requirements for hard skills, such as analytical, mathematical, problem solving and vigilance skills.

The first conversation can thus focus on the dual responsibility for employability. For many, working from home is a major professional transition which must be managed on both the individual and

---

organisational level. How will staff empowerment happen if we cannot follow the principle of "promoting for expertise"?[118] We have to consider new and different competency frameworks and make available mentorship – not only job-related, but also for coping with "new normal" demands. Talent management frameworks will face increasing challenges, and consideration will increasingly focus on the retention of talent. Furthermore, remuneration frameworks, especially under changed working conditions, continue to be readjusted – notably with regard to cost-efficiency and organisational sustainability.

Secondly, the typical employee life cycle and accompanying human resource activities are changing. The employee life cycle consists of two major themes: performance monitoring (issues related to motivation and engagement) as well as interventions that might be required to address monotony and disengagement.[119] Conversations will increasingly centre on the orientation of employees and helping them settle in, as the workplace has become – and will remain – scattered. When employees are consciously competent and confident, high levels of affective commitment are evident. At this stage, development initiatives usually taper off and commitment might become more normative, to the point where employees feel obliged to stay with their employer. Conversations will centre on adjustments to human resources practices so that performance, motivation and engagement remain high.

The next two stages in the employee life-cycle (monotony and disengagement) often unfold when employees become comfortable and job performance is automated. Mello noted that this sets in three to seven years after appointment, however the current situation may have impacted this greatly.[120] Commitment often becomes more continuous in that employees feel obliged to stay with their organisation, often because of a lack of opportunities and their financial obligations. In addition, workplace emergency interventions such as retrenchments, pay cuts and different working arrangements could prompt monotony and disengagement to emerge earlier in employee life cycles. Human resources practitioners are challenged to identify employees' intentions to resign early, and then consider how they could (often remotely) remain visible and involved.

Conversation 2: Rethinking the people-organisation relationship

Changes in the business environment due to 4IR and Covid-19 have a profound impact on the people-organisation relationship. In addition, the work location has changed, influencing people's experience of work, the psychological contract and their work commitment, as well as their overall health and mental wellness. It must be considered that organisations' self-image and pride have been affected.

Increased attention must be paid to people during times of crises, especially to identify opportunity costs for employees.[121] The psychological attachment and presence of employees have been severed by Covid-19. Veldsman and Coetzee[122] described psychological attachment as a "sense of organisational commitment, work absorption and intrinsic motivation", whilst the challenge is how employees will recover. They further elaborated on psychological work immersion, saying that it, amongst others, involves physical identification with the organisation. The importance of the physical environment was already acknowledged in 1984 by Gilmore and Hirschhorn, insofar that workplaces become scattered when people work from home. The question is thus how physical space will be consolidated into a more cohesive future identity.

It is interesting that when employees think of themselves as survivors – given job cuts and the challenges organisations face today – this has an impact on their relationship with, and attitude towards, their organisation.[123]

Conversation 3: Relooking employment contracts, HR policies and frameworks

Working from home, telecommuting and extreme flexibility in working arrangements have become a permanent feature in organisations. Altig et al.[124] reported that working from home as an employee option is expected to triple in the U.S. – there is no reason to believe that it should be different for us. Compressed work schedules and job sharing will also be the order of the day.[125] The high percentage of job losses, business closures, reorganisations and restructurings demand a renewal of traditional employment contracts, HR policies and frameworks. However, Barrero, Bloom and Davis[126] highlighted that these also present opportunities to both employees and organisations for potential beneficial reforms. Typical conversation prompts will include a redefinition of work and the organisation, as well as human resources policies and procedures for the future.

Conversation 4: Rebuilding morale, wellness and productivity

Several authors and public authorities have cautioned organisations about the potential impact of Covid-19 on staff's mental health.[127, 128] Van Hoof[129] warned that burnout and stress-related absenteeism could increase rapidly during the latter half of 2020. Examples of typical symptoms of mental health problems are psychological stress, anxiety, anger, boredom, post-traumatic stress symptoms and depression.[130] From an organisational point of view, job losses are "painful for all involved", and even those who retain their jobs still experience several psychological challenges.[131]

A conversation prompt is the consideration of rebuild morale; it is of paramount importance to focus on staff's emotions which are socially constructed and thus, amongst others, dependent on social relations.[132] The affective event that triggered the negative impact on morale was the pandemic, resulting in a fear of job cuts, increased probability of illness and financial losses, as well as more demands for psychological coping.[133] Herriot put it clearly: "the future of work is largely synonymous with the future of the employment relationship".[134]

One of the most critical questions will centre on how to overcome so-called 'zombieism', which is described as a life devoid of meaning and energy, with no connection to the organisation's mission and values. 'Zombies' are characterised by being normatively committed to their organisations, but there is high evidence of counterproductive work behaviours.[135] Organisations and their human resources departments must actively engage in creating hopefulness, focusing on performance and outputs. As Turner pointed out: we receive what we measure, and we measure what is significant to us.[136] Ultimately, we need to question what we are overvaluing that provokes zombeism.

A first conversation prompt is: how are we going to contribute to create meaningful work for employees?[137] Trevor referred to artificial intelligence as "an indispensable core organisational resource".[138] Both Trevor and Wilson and Daugherty,[139, 140] emphasised that people and technological resources will work more hand-in-hand in the future. Job design has to take cognisance that "authentic delegation" will be more prominent, providing more opportunity for people to take risks, as well as providing innovation opportunities.[141]

Conversation 5: Innovative work design methods

It is increasingly challenging to entertain the notion of well-designed and well-defined jobs. Traditional job or work design models do not necessarily address job design requirements for a "new normal" in a sufficient manner. It must be taken into consideration that new work arrangements require new routines and habits.[142, 143, 144] Work design methods must endeavour to achieve flow in work – otherwise known as workflow, which is defined as: "the total attention and psychic energy devoted to the task in hand, and feelings of exhilaration, comfort and energy that is described as a positive affective state".[145] The challenge is that workflow disruption results in pressure on both productivity and output.[146] For now, one could consider adjusting the actual workflow and managerial expectations to compensate for employees' experiences of emotional and cognitive fatigue. This challenge is exacerbated by the temporariness of the situation.[147] Ulrich and Brookband also emphasised flow as important for goal achievement.[148] They described flow in terms of *who* (ownership of tasks), *how* (work methods) and *where* (place of work). Synergy is achieved when all individual efforts are combined.

Garg and Rastogi proposed that flow can be achieved through effective job design when:

Match between the Individual's		Total Attention and Psychic		
	→	Energy Devoted to the	→	State of "FLOW"
Perceived Skills and Tasks		Task		

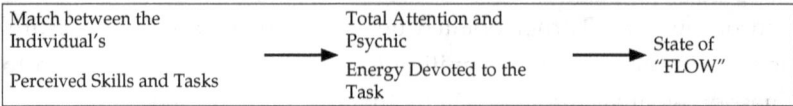

Figure 10.1: Effective job design outcomes[149]

10.2 CONCLUSION

In all aspects of job design, Job Evaluation and remuneration decisions, now more than ever, we should adhere to "principles of fairness, wellness and integrity".[150] Organisations have to re-imagine their business, especially to co-create the deployment of AI technologies and optimise collaborative intelligence.[151]

Human resources practices are challenged more than ever before to add value to people. Ulrich and Brookbank[152] recommended that flow of people, performance management and work be reconsidered in this regard. Trevor advised that organisations identify core people attributes, that is, "competencies, behaviours, knowledge and effort of both individuals and groups that provide for sustainability and competitive advantage".[153] Organisational structures, and arguably, job design, must empower and enable people to perform. This implies a reconsideration of hierarchical control.[154]

Annexures

Annexure 1: Commonly used systems of Job Evaluation

21st CENTURY 7 LEVEL BROADBAND	21st CENTURY EXECU-MEASURE	SST	PATERSON BROAD-BAND	PATERSON	POINTS	PEROMNES	TASK	HAY (typical application)	REWARD LEVELS	REMEASURE	JE MANAGER (typical application)	EQUATE	Mercer IPE Position Class	Towers Watson Grading Application
P (Primary Skills)														
Unskilled				A1	5	19/18	1	54 – 62 (57)	4	20 - 29	1 – 7	1	40	1
Basic Skilled		Low 1		A2	6	17	2	63 – 72 (66)	5	30 - 39	8 – 16	2	41	1
Higher Skilled			A	A3	7	16	3	73 – 84 (75)	6	40 - 49	17 – 24	3		1
O (Operational)														
Basic Operational Skills			B Lower	B1	8	15	4	85 – 97 (90)	7	50 - 59	25 – 34	4	42	2
				B2	9	14	5	98 – 113 (104)	8	60 - 69	35 – 44	5	43	3
Mid-Level Operational Skills		Mid 1	B Mid	B3	10	13	6	114 – 134 (125)	9	70 - 79	45 – 54	5	44	4
			B Upper	B4	11	12	7	135 – 160 (151)	10	80 - 89	55 – 64	6	45	5
High Level Operational Skills				B5	12	12	8	161 – 191 (173)	11	90 - 99	65 – 74	7		6

21st CENTURY 7 LEVEL BROADBAND	21st CENTURY EXECU-MEASURE	SST	PATERSON BROAD-BAND	PATERSON	PATERSON POINTS	PEROMNES	TASK	HAY (typical application)	REWARD LEVELS	REMEASURE	JE MANAGER (typical application)	EQUATE	Mercer IPE Position Class	Towers Watson Grading Application
AO (Advanced Operational)	AOS (Advanced Operational Specialist)													
Advanced Skills			C Lower	C1	13	11	9	192 – 227 (208)	12	100 - 109	75 – 84	7	46	7
Advanced Operational Skills	Qualified Artisan	High 1		C2	14	10	10	228 – 268 (252)	13	110 - 119	85 – 94	8	47	8
Advanced Operational Checking	Entry Level Specialist	Low 2	C Mid	C3	15	9	11	269 – 313 (291)	14	120 - 129	95 – 104	9	48/49	9
L (Leader)	S (Specialist)													
Supervisor/ Team Leader Single Team	Certified Specialist	Mid 2	C Upper	C4	16	8	12	314 – 370 (342)	15	130 - 139	105 – 114	10	50	10
	Practitioner	High 2		C5	17	7	13	314 – 370 (342)	15	140 - 149	115 – 124	11	51/52	11
M (Manager/ Head Of)	P (Professional/ Consultant)													
Technician/ Team Leader Multiple Teams	Entry Level Cons/ High Level Technician	Low 3	D Lower	D1	18	7	14	371 – 438 (406)	16	150 - 159	125 – 134	11	53	12
Middle Management	Professional			D2	19	6	15	439 – 518 (479)	17	160 - 169	135 – 144	12	54	13
Tactical Optimisation	"Qualified" Consultant	Mid 3	D Mid	D3	20	5	16	519 – 613 (571)	18	170 - 179	145 – 154	13	55/56	14

21st CENTURY 7 LEVEL BROADBAND	21st CENTURY EXECU-MEASURE	SST	PATERSON BROAD-BAND	PATERSON	PATERSON POINTS	PEROMNES	TASK	HAY (typical application)	REWARD LEVELS	REMEASURE	JE MANAGER (typical application)	EQUATE	Mercer IPE Position Class	Towers Watson Grading Application
	3rd Level Specialist													
	Highest Level Consultant	High 3	D Upper	D4	21	5	17	614 – 734 (677)	19	180 - 189	155 – 164	13	57/58	15
				D5	22	4	18	614 – 734 (677)	19	190 - 199	165 – 174	14	59	15
SE (Strategic Execution)	SE (Professional)													
	Organisation/ Distinctive Authority Abstract/ Strategic Research	22 Low 4	E Lower	E1	23	4	18	735 – 879 (805)	20	200 - 209	175 – 184	14	60/61	16
Senior Management	Experienced Professional	23 Mid 4		E2	24	3	19	880 – 1055 (954)	21	210 - 219	185 – 194	15	62	17
Strategy Execution	Recog authority in industry/specialist field	24 High 4	E Mid	E3	25	3	20	1056 – 1260 (1142)	22	220 - 229	195 – 204	15	63/64	18
SI (Strategic Intent)														
National Authority/Rare Authority	26	25 Low 5	E Upper	E4	26	2	21	1261 – 1507 (1372)	23	230 - 239	205 – 214	16	65	19
				E5	27	2	22	1508 – 1800 (1628)	24	240 - 249	215 – 224	16	66/67	20
Sometimes International	27		F Lower	F1	28	1	23	1801 – 2140 (1960)	25	250 - 259	225 – 234	16	68	21

21st CENTURY 7 LEVEL BROADBAND	21st CENTURY EXECU-MEASURE	SST	PATERSON BROAD-BAND	PATERSON	PATERSON POINTS	PEROMNES	TASK	HAY (typical application)	REWARD LEVELS	REMEASURE	JE MANAGER (typical application)	EQUATE	Mercer IPE Position Class	Towers Watson Grading Application
	28			F2	29	1	24	2141 – 2550 (2328)	26	260 - 269	235 - 244	16	69	
Top Management (usually Board level), strategic intent and policy making decisions	29	Mid 5	F Mid	F3	30	1+	25	2141 – 2550 (2328)	26	270 - 279	245 – 254		70	
	30	High 5	F Upper	F4	31	1+	26	2551 - 3020 (2812)	27	280 - 298	255 – 264		71 and above	
	31			F5	32	1+		3021 - 3580 (3232)	28	290 - 299	265 – 275			
G-Global Corporate Governance														
Global Corporate Governance (Minimal Board Influence) - Oversee	32	Low 6		G1				3581 - 5060 (4321)					74	22
		Mid 6	G Lower	G2									76	23
Complex Systems: Cross-national and global-regional strategy and direction formulation. There is minimal board influence	33	High 6		G3				5061 - 6020 (5541)						

21st CENTURY 7 LEVEL BROADBAND	21st CENTURY EXECU-MEASURE	SST	PATERSON BROAD-BAND	PATERSON PATERSON POINTS	PEROMNES	TASK	HAY (typical application)	REWARD LEVELS	REMEASURE	JE MANAGER (typical application)	EQUATE	Mercer IPE Position Class	Towers Watson Grading Application
Global Corporate Governance - Construct Complex Systems: Cross-national and global strategy and direction formulation. Determining of overall multi-national organisations strategy and direction. Often owns a major share of the group. No other influence other than legal and public interest	34	Low 7	G Upper	G4			6021 - 9640 (7831)					78	24
		Mid 7		G5									
		High 7		G6									

133

REFERENCES

Chapter 1 References

Bostwick, J. 2016. *Global business trends to watch for in 2016*. Available from: https://www.radiusworldwide.com/blog/2016/1/global-business-trends-watch-2016

Bremmer, I. & Kupchan, C. 2017. *TopRisks 2017: The Geopolitical Recession*. New York: Eurasia Group.

Bremmer, I. 2015. *These are the Top 10 Geopolitical Risks of 2015*. Available from: http://time.com/3652421/geopolitical-risks-2015-ian-bremmer-eurasia-group/

Cheese, P., Silverstone, Y. & Smith, D.Y. 2009. Creating an agile organisation. *Outlook Journal of Accenture, 3*: 1-6.

Global Business Policy Council. 2016. *12 Global Trends to Watch in 2016*. Available from: https://www.linkedin.com/pulse/twelve-key-global-trends-watch-2016-erik-peterson

Havemann, Y., Beyers, C. & Finch, J. 2014. *Key Challenges to Drive Business Performance*. Johannesburg: inavit iQ.

IMF. 2020. *World Economic Outlook Update, June 2020*. Available from: https://www.imf.org/en/Publications/WEO/Issues/2020/06/24/WEOUpdateJune2020

International Labour Organisation (ILO). 2016. *World Employment Social Outlook: Trends 2016*. Available from: http://www.ilo.org/global/research/global-reports/weso/2016/lang--en/index.htm

Kaiser, E. 2015. *5 Ways Millennials will change the American Work Place*. Available from: http://www.mprnews.org/story/2015/05/27/bcst-recent-graduates-workforce

Morgan, J. 2014. *Why the collaborative economy is changing everything*. Available from: http://www.forbes.com/sites/jacobmorgan/2014/10/16/why-the-collaborative-economy-is-changing-everything/#4540f2b24fc1

Parker, A.J. 1998. *The role of employment relations management in the business strategy of South African organisation's pursuit of 'world-class'* (Master's dissertation). Johannesburg: RAU.

Reuben, A. 2015. *Gap between rich and poor 'keeps growing'*. Available from: http://www.bbc.com/news/business-32824770

Setili, A. 2014. *The Agility Advantage: How to Identify and Act on Opportunities in a Fast-Changing World*. San Francisco: Jossey-Bass.

Standage, T. 16 Nov 2020. Ten trends to watch in the coming year. *The Economist*. Available from: https://www.economist.com/the-world-ahead/2020/11/16/ten-trends-to-watch-in-the-coming-year

Uzialko, A.C. 2017. *40 Small business trends and predictions for 2017*. Available from: https://www.sitecore.com/ja-jp/company/news-events/news/2017/01/40-small-business-trends-and-predictions-for-2017

World Economic Forum. 2016a. *Internet Fragmentation: An Overview.* Available from: http://www.weforum.org/reports/internet-fragmentation-an-overview

World Economic Forum. 2016b. *Digital Media and Society implications in a hyperconnected era.* Available from: http://www3.weforum.org/docs/WEFUSA_DigitalMediaAndSociety_Report2016.pdf

World Economic Forum. 2016c. *The Global Risks Report* (11th ed.). Available from: http://www3.weforum.org/docs/GRR/WEF_GRR16.pdf

World Economic Forum. 2017. *The Global Risks Report* (12th ed.). Available from: http://www3.weforum.org/docs/GRR17_Report_web.pdf

Chapter 2 References

Beeline. 2021. *The Biggest Risks in Your Contingent Workforce Program (and How to Mitigate Them).* Available from: https://www.beeline.com/blog/biggest-risks-contingent-workforce-program-mitigate/

Crous, W. 2018. *The Move towards Agile and Agile HR.* Blog article.

Freelance Platform. 2021. Best *Freelance Platforms.* Available from: https://www.g2crowd.com/categories/freelance-platforms

Manyika, J., Lund, S., Robinson, K., Valentino, J. & Dobbs, R. 2015. *Connecting talent with opportunity in the digital age.* Available from: https://www.mckinsey.com/featured-insights/employment-and-growth/connecting-talent-with-opportunity-in-the-digital-age

Muldowney, S. 2019. *The rise of the contingent workforce.* Available from: https://insightsresources.seek.com.au/rise-contingent-workforce-attracting-managing-engaging-transient-staff

OCG A Chandler Macleod Group Company. 2017. *The Rise of the Contingent Workforce.* Available from: https://www.prominence.social/wp-content/uploads/2017/01/OCG-Contingent-Whitepaper-No-Bleed.pdf

PeopleTicker. 2017. *History of Contingent Labor: Welcoming a New, Elastic Workforce.* Available from: http://www.peopleticker.com/news/history-of-contingent-labor-welcoming-a-new-elastic-workforce

Rampton. J. 2017. *Employers Are Paying Freelancers Big Bucks for These 25 In-Demand Skills.* Available from: https://www.entrepreneur.com/article/294718

Reber, A.S. 1985. *The Penguin Dictionary of Psychology.* New York: Penguin Publishing Group.

Roy, M. 2016. *Contingent Workforce.* Available from: https://searchcio.techtarget.com/definition/contingent-workforce

Wikipedia. 2021a. *Fiverr.* Available from: https://en.wikipedia.org/wiki/Fiverr

Wikipedia. 2021b. *Freelancer.* Available from: https://en.wikipedia.org/wiki/Freelancer.com

Wikipedia. 2021c. *Upwork.* Available from: https://en.wikipedia.org/wiki/Upwork

Wikipedia. 2021d. Employment. Available from: https://en.wikipedia.org/wiki/Employment

Chapter 3 References

Bussin, M. 2020. *The Remuneration Handbook for Africa. Fourth edition*. Randburg: KR Publishing.

Chapter 6 References

Baldridge, D.C., Beatty, J.E., Konrad, A.M. & Moore, M.E. 2016. People with disabilities. In: R. Bendl, I. Bleijenbergh, E. Henttonen & A.J. Mills. *The Oxford Handbook of Diversity in Organizations*. Oxford: Oxford University Press, p469–498.

Barzilay, A.R. & Ben-David, A. 2017. Platform Inequality: Gender in the Gig-Economy. *Seton Hall Law Review*, 47(2), 393-431.

Cook, C., Diamond, R., Hall, J., List, J.A. & Oyer, P. 2018. *The Gender Earnings Gap in the Gig Economy: Evidence from Over a Million Rideshare Drivers*. The National Bureau of Economic Research Working Paper No. 24732. Available at: https://www.gsb.stanford.edu/faculty-research/working-papers/gender-earnings-gap-gig-economy-evidence-over-million-rideshare

Eurostat. 2017. *Disability statistics*. Available at: http://ec.europa.eu/eurostat/statistics-explained/index.php?title=Disability_statistics. Accessed 2 September 2018.

Gonzalez-Rodriguez, M.R., Martin-Samper, R.C., Koseoglu, M.A. & Okumus, F. 2019. Hotel's corporate social responsibility practices, organizational culture, firm reputation, and performance. *Journal of Sustainable Tourism*, 27(3): 398-419.

ILO. 2018. *Global Wage Report 2018/19: What lies behind gender pay gaps*. Geneva, Switzerland: International Labour Office.

Job Accommodation Network (JAN). 2019. *Workplace accommodations: Low cost, high impact*. Available from: https://askjan.org/topics/costs.cfm<

Kraus, L. 2017. *2016 disability statistics annual report*. Durham: University of New Hampshire.

World Economic Forum. 2021. *Global Gender Gap Report*. Geneva, Switzerland.

Chapter 7 References

Azam, J.P. & Rospabe, S. 2005. *Trade Unions vs Statistical Discrimination: Theory and Application to Post-Apartheid South Africa*. Toulouse: University of Toulouse.

Casale, D. & Posle, D. 2010. Unions and the Gender Wage Gap in South Africa. *Journal of African Economies*, 20(1): 27-59.

Chiu, R., Luk, V. & Tang, T. 2000. Pay Differentials in the People's Republic of China: An Examination of Internal Equity and External Competitiveness, Compensation and Benefits Review. *Sage Journal*, 32: 58.

De Gregorio, J. & Lee, J. 2002. Education and Income Inequality: New Evidence from Cross-Country Data. *Review of Income and Wealth*, 48(3): 395-414.

Department of Labour. 1998. *Employment Equity Act, No. 55 of 1998*. South Africa. Available from: *http://labour.gov.za*

Department of Labour. 2014. *Employment Equity Act, No. 55 of 1998 (as amended), Draft Code of Good Practice on Equal Pay for Work of Equal Value"*. Government Gazette No. 38031, 29 September 2014.

Helpman, E., Itskhoki, O. & Redding, S. 2009. *Inequality and Unemployment in a Global Economy*. Centre for Economic Performance Discussion Paper No. 940.

Leibbrandt, M., Finn, A. & Woolard, I. 2012. Describing and Decomposing Post-Apartheid Income Inequality in South Africa. *Development Southern Africa*, 29(1): 19-34. Available from http://www.tandfonline.com/loi/cdsa20

Mostafa, E., Saeed, S. & Samira, P. 2014. Income Inequality and Health in Organization of Islamic Countries. *Journal of Macroeconomics*, 9(17): 141-160.

Solt, F. 2008. *Standardising the World Income Inequality Database*. Luxembourg Income Study Working Paper Series No. 496.

Chapter 9 References

Fineman, S. 2006. Emotion and Organizing. In Clegg, S.R., Hardy, C., Lawrence, T.B. & Nord, W.R. (Eds). *The Sage Handbook of Organization Studies* (2nd ed.). London: Sage Publications, pp. 675-700.

Firth, R. 1989. Write a job description. *British Medical Journal* 298(1): 1306-7.

Oldham, G.R. & Hackman, J.R. 2010. *Not what it was and not what it will be: the future of job design research*. Journal of Organizational Behavior, 3(2-3): 463-479.

Hackman, J.R. & Oldham, G.R. 1976. Motivation through the design of work: Test of a theory. *Organizational Behavior and Human Performance*, 16(2): 250-279.

Hodgson, P. & Crainer, S. 1993. *What do high performance managers really do?* London: Pitman.

Kalleberg, A.L. 2008. The mismatched worker: When people don't fit their jobs. *Academy of Management Perspectives* 22(1), 24-40.

Maddux, J.E. 2009. Self-efficacy: The power of believing you can. In Lopez, S.J. & Snyder, C.R. (eds). *The Oxford Handbook of Positive Psychology*, (2nd ed.). New York, New York: Oxford University Press, pp. 335-342.

Mello, J.A. 2015. *Strategic human resource management* (4th ed.). Stamford, United States: Cengage Learning.

Meyer, M., Roodt, G. & Robbins, M. 2011. Human resources risk management: Governing people risks for improved performance. *SA Journal of Human Resource Management* 9(1): a366.

Moerdyk, A., Dodd, N., Donald, F., Kiley, J., Van Hoek, G. & Van Hoek, L. 2018. *Organisational Behaviour*. Cape Town: Oxford University Press.

Morgenson, F.P. & Humphrey, S.E. 2006. The Work Design Questionnaire (WDQ): Developing and Validating a Comprehensive Measure for Assisting Job Design and the Nature of Work. *Journal of Applied Psychology*, 91: 1321-1339. https://doi.org/10.1037/0021-9010.91.6.1321

Mullins, L.J. & McClean, J. 2019. *Organisational behaviour in the workplace* (12th ed.). Harlow, United Kingdom: Pearson Education Limited.

Oldham, G.R. & Hackman, J.R. 2010. *Not what it was and not what it will be: the future of job design research.* Journal of Organizational Behavior, 3(2-3): 463-479.

Robbins, S.R. & Judge, T.A. 2019. *Organizational Behaviour* (18th ed.). Harlow, UK: Pearson Education Limited.

Schwab, K. & Davis, N. 2018. *Shaping the Future of the Fourth Industrial Revolution.* London: Penguin Random House.

Siddique, C. 2004. Job Analysis: A Strategic Human Resource Management Practice. *The International Journal of Human Resource Management*, 15: 219-244, https//doi.org/10.1080/0958519032000157438

Singh, P. 2008. Job analysis for a changing workplace. *Human Resource Management Review, 18*(2): 87-99.

Wilson, M.A. 2007. A history of job analysis. In Koppes, L.L. (ed). *Historical perspectives in industrial and organizational psychology.* New York: Psychology Press, pp. 219-241.

Chapter 10 References

Attig, D.E., Barrero, J.M., Bloom, N.J., Davis, J.S., Meyer, B., Mihaylow, E. & Parker, N.B. 2020. *Firms expect working from home to triple.* Available from: https://www.atlantafed.org/blogs/macroblog/2020/05/28/firms-expect-working-from-home-to-triple

Bailey, C., LipsWiersma, M., Madden, A., Yeoman, R., Thompson, M. and Chalofsky, N., 2019. The five paradoxes of meaningful work: Introduction to the special issue 'meaningful work: Prospects for the 21st century'. *Journal of Management Studies, 56*(3), pp.481-499.

Barrero, J.M., Bloom, N. & Davis, S.J. 2020. COVID-19 is also a reallocation shock. *National Bureau of Economic Research* Working Pager 27137.

Garg, P. & Rastogi, R. 2006. New model of job design: motivation employees' performance. *Journal of Management Development, 25*(6): 572-587. Doi: 10.1108/02621710610570137.

Gilmore, T.N. & Hirschhorn, L. 1984. Managing human resources in a declining context. In Fombrun, C.J., Tichy, N.M. & Devanna, M.A. (eds). *Strategic Human Resource Management*. New York: John Wiley & Sons, pp. 297-318.

Hacker, S. 2010. Zombies in the Workplace. *The Journal for Quality and Participation, 32*(4): 25-28.

Herriot, P. 2001. *The Employment Relationship: A Psychological Perspective.* London: Routledge.

Hodgson, P. & Crainer, S. 1993. *What do high performance managers really do?* London: Pitman, p. 195.

Kar S.K., Yasir Arafat S.M., Kabir R., Sharma P. & Saxena S.K. 2020. Coping with Mental Health Challenges During COVID-19. In Saxena S. (ed). *Coronavirus Disease 2019 (COVID-19). Medical Virology: From Pathogenesis to Disease Control.* Singapore: Springer. https://doi.org/10.1007/978-981-15-4814-7_16

Kwon, K. & Park, J. 2019. The life cycle of employee engagement theory in HRD research. *Advances in Developing Human Resources 21*(3): 352-370. Doi: 10.1177/152342239851443.

Mello, J.A. 2015. *Strategic human resource management* (4th ed.). Stamford, United States: Cengage Learning.

Mention, A-L., Ferreira, J.J.P. & Torkkeli, M. 2020. Coronavirus: a catalyst for change and innovation. *Journal of Innovation Management 8*(1): 1-5. Doi: https://doi.org/1024840/2183-0606_001-0001.

Mullins, L.J. & McClean, J. 2019. *Organisational behaviour in the workplace* (12th ed.). Harlow, United Kingdom: Pearson Education Limited.

Takieddine, H. & Al Tabbah, S. 2020. Coronavirus Pandemic: Coping with the Psychological outcomes, mental changes, and the "new normal" during and after COVID-19. *Open Journal of Depression and Anxiety, 2:* 1-7. Doi: https://doi.org/10.36811/ojda/2020.110005.

Torales, J., O'Higgins, M., Castaldeili-Maia, J.M. & Ventriglo, A. 2020. The outbreak of COVID-19 coronavirus and its impact on global mental health. *International Journal of Social Psychiatry, 66*(4): 317-320.

Trevor, J. 2019. *Align: A Leadership Blueprint for Aligning Enterprise Purpose, Strategy and Organization: A Leadership Blueprint for Aligning Enterprise Purpose, Strategy and Organisation.* London: Bloomsbury Business, pp. 161-163.

Turner, D.P. 2020. Sampling Methods in Research Design. *Headache The Journal of Head and Face Pain, 60*(1): 8-12.

Ulrich, D. & Brookbank, W. 2005. *The HR Value Proposition.* Boston, MA: Harvard Business School Press.

Van Hoof, E. 2020. *Lockdown is the world's biggest psychological experiment – and we will pay the price.* Available from: https://www.weforum.org/agenda/2020/04/this-is-the-psychologic

Veldsman, D. & Coetzee, M. 2014. People performance enablers in relation to employees' psychological attachment to the organisation. *Journal of Psychology in Africa, 24*(6): 480-486. Doi: 10.1080/14330237.2014.997028.

Wilson, H.J. and Daugherty, P.R., 2018. Collaborative intelligence: Humans and AI are joining forces. *Harvard Business Review, 96*(4), pp.114-123.

World Health Organization. 2020. *Mental health and psychosocial considerations during the COVID-19 outbreak.* Available from: https://www.who.int/docs/default-source/coronaviruse/mental-health-considerations.pdf

Zucker, R. 2020. Managers, adjust your expectations (without lowering the bar). *Harvard Business Review*, May: 2-4. Available from: https://hbr.org/2020/05/managers-adjust-your-expectations-without-lowering-the-bar

ENDNOTES

1   World Economic Forum. 2017. *The Global Risks Report* (12th ed.). Available from: http://www3.weforum.org/docs/GRR17_Report_web.pdf

2   World Economic Forum. 2016b. *Digital Media and Society implications in a hyperconnected era.* Available from: http://www3.weforum.org/docs/WEFUSA_DigitalMediaAndSociety_Report2016.pdf

3   Ibid.

4   Bostwick, J. 2016. *Global business trends to watch for in 2016.* Available from: https://www.radiusworldwide.com/blog/2016/1/global-business-trends-watcCBh-2016

5   Bremmer, I. 2015. *These are the Top 10 Geopolitical Risks of 2015.* Available from: http://time.com/3652421/geopolitical-risks-2015-ian-bremmer-eurasia-group/

6   Ibid.

7   International Labour Organisation (ILO). 2016. *World Employment Social Outlook: Trends 2016.* Available from: http://www.ilo.org/global/research/global-reports/weso/2016/lang--en/index.htm.

8   Ibid.

9   Global Business Policy Council. 2016. *12 Global Trends to Watch in 2016.* Available from: https://www.linkedin.com/pulse/twelve-key-global-trends-watch-2016-erik-peterson

10 Morgan, J. 2014. *Why the collaborative economy is changing everything.* Available from: http://www.forbes.com/sites/jacobmorgan/2014/10/16/why-the-collaborative-economy-is-changing-everything/#4540f2b24fc1

11 World Economic Forum, 2017.

12 Reuben, A. 2015. *Gap between rich and poor 'keeps growing'.* Available from: http://www.bbc.com/news/business-32824770

13 Ibid.

14 ILO, 2016.

15 Ibid.

16 Kaiser, E. 2015. *5 Ways Millennials will change the American Work Place.* Available from: http://www.mprnews.org/story/2015/05/27/bcst-recent-graduates-workforce

17 Uzialko, A.C. 2017. *40 Small business trends and predictions for 2017.* Available from: https://www.sitecore.com/ja-jp/company/news-events/news/2017/01/40-small-business-trends-and-predictions-for-2017

18 World Economic Forum. 2016c. *The Global Risks Report* (11th ed.). Available from: http://www3.weforum.org/docs/GRR/WEF_GRR16.pdf

19 World Economic Forum. 2022. *The Global Risks Report 2022* (17th ed.). Available from: https://www3.weforum.org/docs/WEF_The_Global_Risks_Report_2022.pdf

20 Orchard, P. 2020. *Assessing the economic effects of the coronavirus.* Available from: https://geopoliticalfutures.com/assessing-the-economic-effects-of-the-coronavirus/

21 Maréchal, M.A., Kube, S. & Puppe, C. 2013. Do wage cuts damage work morale? Evidence from a natural field experiment. *Journal of the European Economic Association*, 11(4): 853-870.

22 Shelton, A.M. 2010. *Compensated work sharing arrangements (short-term compensation) as an alternative to layoffs.* Congressional Research Services. Available from: https://www.everycrsreport.com/files/20100203_R40689_1fddbb3a8fbe7008fdbdba79e6b36d8697722bc8.pdf

23 Kiviat, B. 2009. *After Layoffs, There's Survivor's Guilt. In Shelton, A.M. Compensated work sharing arrangements (short-term compensation) as an alternative to layoffs.* Congressional Research Services. Available from: https://www.everycrsreport.com/files/20100203_R40689_1fddbb3a8fbe7008fdbdba79e6b36d8697722bc8.pdf

24 Shelton, 2010, p. 9.

25 Singh, A. & Gupta, B. (2015). Job involvement, organizational commitment, professional commitment, and team commitment: A study of generational diversity. *Benchmarking*, 22(6): 1192–1211.

26 Isenhour, L.C. 2006. *The relations among cultural values, ethnicity, and job choice trade-off preferences.* Unpublished doctoral dissertation. Florida: University of Central Florida.

27 Bussin, M. 2017. *Organisation design in Uber times.* Randburg: Knowledge Resources. ISBN: 9781869227098.

28 Parker, A.J. 1998. *The role of employment relations management in the business strategy of South African organisation's pursuit of 'world-class'* (Master's dissertation). Johannesburg: RAU.

29 The Economist. 2020. *The changes COVID-19 is forcing onto business.* Available from: https://www.economist.com/briefing/2020/04/11/the-changes-covid-19-is-forcing-on-to-business

30 Ibid.

31 Crous, W. 2018. *The Move towards Agile and Agile HR.* Randburg: KR Publishing.

32 Wikipedia. 2021a. *Fiverr.* Available from: https://en.wikipedia.org/wiki/Fiverr

33 Wikipedia. 2021b. *Freelancer.* Available from: https://en.wikipedia.org/wiki/Freelancer.com

34 Wikipedia. 2021c. *Upwork.* Available from: https://en.wikipedia.org/wiki/Upwork

35 Wikipedia. 2021d. *Employment.* Available from: https://en.wikipedia.org/wiki/Employment

36 Roy, M. 2016. *Contingent Workforce.* Available from: https://searchcio.techtarget.com/definition/contingent-workforce

37 South African Government. 1996. Labour Relations Act 66 of 1995. Pretoria: Government Printers.

38 OCG A Chandler Macleod Group Company. 2017. *The Rise of the Contingent Workforce.* Available from: https://www.prominence.social/wp-content/uploads/2017/01/OCG-Contingent-Whitepaper-No-Bleed.pdf

39   PeopleTicker. 2017. *History of Contingent Labor: Welcoming a New, Elastic Workforce*. Available from: http://www.peopleticker.com/news/history-of-contingent-labor-welcoming-a-new-elastic-workforce

40   Manyika, J., Lund, S., Robinson, K., Valentino, J. & Dobbs, R. 2015. *Connecting talent with opportunity in the digital age*. Available from: https://www.mckinsey.com/featured-insights/employment-and-growth/connecting-talent-with-opportunity-in-the-digital-age

41   Rampton. J. 2017. *Employers Are Paying Freelancers Big Bucks for These 25 In-Demand Skills*. Available from: https://www.entrepreneur.com/article/294718

42   Reber, A.S. 1985. *The Penguin Dictionary of Psychology*. New York: Penguin Publishing Group.

43   Bussin, M. & Blair, C. 2018. *The New World of Work - an SOS call to Management*. Randburg: Knowledge Resources.

44   OCG A Chandler Macleod Group Company. 2017. *The Rise of the Contingent Workforce*. Available from: https://www.prominence.social/wp-content/uploads/2017/01/OCG-Contingent-Whitepaper-No-Bleed.pdf

45   Muldowney, S. 2019. *The rise of the contingent workforce*. Available from: https://insightsresources.seek.com.au/rise-contingent-workforce-attracting-managing-engaging-transient-staff

46   Ibid.

47   OCG A Chandler Macleod Group Company, 2017.

48   Deloitte. 2013. *Contingent Workforce*. Available from: https://www2.deloitte.com/za/en/pages/human-capital/articles/contingent-workforce.html

49   Beeline. 2021. *The Biggest Risks in Your Contingent Workforce Program (and How to Mitigate Them)*. Available from: https://www.beeline.com/blog/biggest-risks-contingent-workforce-program-mitigate/

50   Bussin, M. 2020. *The Remuneration Handbook for Africa* (4th ed.). Randburg: KR Publishing.

51   ILO. 2018. *Global Wage Report 2018/19: What lies behind gender pay gaps*. Geneva: International Labour Office.

52   Kraus, L. 2017. *2016 disability statistics annual report*. Durham: University of New Hampshire.

53   Eurostat. 2017. *Disability statistics*. Available at: http://ec.europa.eu/eurostat/statistics-explained/index.php?title=Disability_statistics. Accessed 2 September 2018.

54   Baldridge, D.C., Beatty, J.E., Konrad, A.M. & Moore, M.E. 2016. People with disabilities. In authors. *The Oxford Handbook of Diversity in Organizations*. City: Publisher, pp. 469-498.

55   Cook, C., Diamond, R., Hall, J., List, J.A. & Oyer, P. 2018. *The Gender Earnings Gap in the Gig Economy: Evidence from Over a Million Rideshare Drivers*. The National Bureau of Economic Research Working Paper No. 24732. Available at: https://www.gsb.stanford.edu/faculty-research/working-papers/gender-earnings-gap-gig-economy-evidence-over-million-rideshare

56   Barzilay, A.R. & Ben-David, A. 2017. Platform Inequality: Gender in the Gig-Economy. *Seton Hall Law Review, 47*(2): 393-431.

57   Gonzalez-Rodriguez, M.R., Martin-Samper, R.C., Koseoglu, M.A. & Okumus, F. 2019. Hotel's corporate social responsibility practices, organizational culture, firm reputation, and performance. *Journal of Sustainable Tourism, 27*(3): 398-419.

58   Job Accommodation Network (JAN). 2019. *Workplace accommodations: Low cost, high impact.* Available from: https://askjan.org/topics/costs.cfm<

59   World Economic Forum. 2021. *Global Gender Gap Report.* Geneva: WEF.

60   World Bank Data. 2022. *Gini index* (World Bank estimate) - South Africa. Available from: https://data.worldbank.org/indicator/SI.POV. GINI?locations=ZA

61   South African Government. 2013. Employment Equity Amendment Act 47 of 2013. Available from: https://www.gov.za/documents/employment-equity-amendment-act

62   Department of Labour. 1998. Employment Equity Act, No. 55 of 1998. Available from: http://labour.gov.za

63   The Employment Equity Amendment Act 47 of 2013 – Section 6.

64   The Employment Equity Amendment Act 47 of 2013 – Schedule 1.

65   Department of Labour, 2014, Government Gazette No. 38031.

66   Mostafa, Saeed & Samira. 2014.

67   World Bank Data averaged between 2005 and 2014. Available from: https://databank.worldbank.org/source/world-development-indicators

68   World Bank Data averaged between 2005 and 2014. Available from: https://databank.worldbank.org/source/world-development-indicators

69   De Gregorio & Lee,.2002.

70   World Bank Data. Available from: https://databank.worldbank.org/ source/world-development-indicators

71   Leibbrandt, Finn & Woolard. 2012; Azam & Rospabe. 2005; Casale & Posle. 2010

72   Leibbrandt, Finn & Woolard. 2012.

73   Azam & Rospabe. 2005.

74   Casale & Posle. 2010.

75   Azam & Rospabe. 2005.

76   Casale & Posle. 2010.

77   Solt. 2008.

78   Ibid.

79   Helpman, Itskhoki & Redding. 2009.

80   Chiu, Luk & Tang. 2000.

81   Siddique, C. 2004. Job Analysis: A Strategic Human Resource Management Practice. *The International Journal of Human Resource Management, 15*: 219-244, https://doi.org/10.1080/0958519032000157438

82   Firth, R. 1989. Write a job description. *British Medical Journal, 298*(1): 1306-7.

83   Singh, P. 2008. Job analysis for a changing workplace. *Human Resource Management Review 18*(2): 87-99.

84   Wilson, M.A. 2007. A history of job analysis. In Koppes, L.L. (ed).
     Historical perspectives in industrial and organizational psychology. New York:
     Psychology Press, pp. 219-241.
85   Ibid.
86   Siddique, C. 2004. Job Analysis: A Strategic Human Resource Management
     Practice. *The International Journal of Human Resource Management, 15*: 219-
     244, https//doi.org/10.1080/0958519032000157438
87   Oldham, G.R. & Hackman, J.R. 2010. Not what it was and not what it will
     be: the future of job design research. *Journal of Organizational Behavior, 3*(2-
     3): 463-479.
88   Ibid.
89   Morgenson, F.P. & Humphrey S.E. 2006. The Work Design Questionnaire
     (WDQ): Developing and Validating a Comprehensive Measure for
     Assisting Job Design and the Nature of Work. *Journal of Applied Psychology,
     91*(6): 1321-1339. https://doi.org/10.1037/0021-9010.91.6.1321
90   Oldman, G.R. & Hackman, J.R. 2010. Not what it was and not what it will
     be: The future of job design research. *Journal of Organizational Behavior,
     31*(2-3): 463-479, DOI:10.1002/job.678.
91   Siddique, C. 2004. Job Analysis: A Strategic Human Resource Management
     Practice. *The International Journal of Human Resource Management, 15*: 219-
     244, https//doi.org/10.1080/0958519032000157438
92   Meyer, M., Roodt, G. & Robbins, M. 2011. Human resources risk
     management: Governing people risks for improved performance. *SA Journal
     of Human Resource Management 9*(1): Art#36. Doi: 10.4102?sajhrm.v9il.366
93   Robbins, S.R. & Judge, TA. 2019. *Organizational Behaviour. 18th edition.
     Global Edition.* Harlow, UK: Pearson Education Limited, p.726.
94   Moerdyk, A., Dodd, N., Donald, F., Kiley, J., Van Hoek, G. & Van Hoek,
     L. 2018. *Organisational Behaviour.* Cape Town, South Africa: Oxford
     University Press.
95   Mello, J.A. 2015. *Strategic human resource management.* 4th edition.
     Stamford, United States: Cengage Learning, p.246.
96   Ibid.
97   Kalleberg, A.L. 2008. The mismatched worker: When people don't fit their
     jobs. *Academy of Management Perspectives 22*(1), 24-40.
98   Oldham, G.R. & Hackman, J.R. 2010. Not what it was and not what it will
     be: the future of job design research. *Journal of Organizational Behavior, 3*(2-
     3): 463-479.
99   Hackman, J.R. & Oldham, G.R. 1976. Motivation through the design of
     work: Test of a theory. *Organizational Behavior and Human Performance,
     16*(2): 250-279.
100 Morgenson, F.P. & Humphrey S.E. 2006. The Work Design Questionnaire
     (WDQ): Developing and Validating a Comprehensive Measure for
     Assisting Job Design and the Nature of Work. *Journal of Applied Psychology,
     91*(6): 1321-1339. https://doi.org/10.1037/0021-9010.91.6.1321

101 Maddux, J.E. 2009. Self-efficacy: The power of believing you can. In Lopez, S.J. & Snyder, C.R. (eds). *The Oxford Handbook of Positive Psychology* (2nd ed.). New York, New York: Oxford University Press, pp. 335-342.

102 Robbins, S.R. & Judge, TA. 2019. *Organizational Behaviour* (18th ed.). Harlow, UK: Pearson Education Limited.

103 Mullins, L.J. & McClean, J. 2019. *Organisational behaviour in the workplace* (12th ed.). Harlow, United Kingdom: Pearson Education Limited.

104 Moerdyk, A., Dodd, N., Donald, F., Kiley, J., Van Hoek, G. & Van Hoek, L. 2018. *Organisational Behaviour*. Cape Town: Oxford University Press.

105 Singh, P. 2008. Job analysis for a changing workplace. *Human Resource Management Review, 18*(2): 87-99.

106 Robbins, S.R. & Judge, TA. 2019. *Organizational Behaviour* (18th ed.). Harlow, UK: Pearson Education Limited.

107 Oldham, G.R. & Hackman, J.R. 2010. Not what it was and not what it will be: the future of job design research. *Journal of Organizational Behavior, 3*(2-3): 463-479.

108 Mullins, L.J. & McClean, J. 2019. *Organisational behaviour in the workplace* (12th ed.). Harlow, United Kingdom: Pearson Education Limited, p. 282.

109 Kalleberg, A.L. 2008. The mismatched worker: When people don't fit their jobs. *Academy of Management Perspectives, 22*(1): 24-40.

110 Hodgson, P. & Crainer, S. 1993. *What do high performance managers really do?* London: Pitman, p. 195.

111 Meyer, M., Roodt, G. & Robbins, M. 2011. Human resources risk management: Governing people risks for improved performance. *SA Journal of Human Resource Management 9*(1): Art#36. Doi: 10.4102?sajhrm. v9il.366

112 Schwab, K. & Davis, N. 2018. *Shaping the Future of the Fourth Industrial Revolution.* London: Penguin Random House.

113 Fineman, S. 2006. Emotion and Organizaing. In Clegg, S.R., Hardy, C., Lawrence, T.B. & Nord, W.R. (eds). *The Sage Handbook of Organization Studies* (2nd ed.). London: Sage Publications, pp. 675-700.

114 Oldham, G.R. & Hackman, J.R. 2010. Not what it was and not what it will be: the future of job design research. *Journal of Organizational Behavior, 3*(2-3): 463-479.

115 Ibid.

116 Hodgson, P. & Crainer, S. 1993. *What do high performance mangers really do?* London: Pitman, p. 195.

117 Kwon, K. & Park, J. 2019. The life cycle of employee engagement theory in HRD research. *Advances in Developing Human Resources 21*(3): 352-370. Doi: 10.1177/152342239851443

118 Garg, P. & Rastogi, R. 2006. New model of job design: motivation employees' performance. *Journal of Management Development, 25*(6): 572-587. Doi: 10. 1108/02621710610570137.

119 Mello, J.A. 2016. *Strategic Human Resource Management* (4th ed.). Boston, MA: Cengage Learning.

120 Ibid.

121 Mullins, L.J. & McClean, J. 2019. *Organisational behaviour in the workplace* (12th ed.). Harlow, United Kingdom: Pearson Education Limited.

122 Veldsman, D. & Coetzee, M. 2014. People performance enablers in relation to employees' psychological attachment to the organisation. *Journal of Psychology in Africa, 24*(6): 480-486. Doi: 10.1080/14330237.2014.997028.

123 Gilmore, T.N. & Hirschhorn, L. 1984. Managing human resources in a declining context. In Fombrun, C.J., Tichy, N.M. & Devanna, M.A. (eds). *Strategic Human Resource Management.* New York: John Wiley & Sons, pp. 297-318.

124 Altig et al. 2020.

125 Garg, P. & Rastogi, R. 2006. New model of job design: motivation employees' performance. *Journal of Management Development, 25*(6): 572-587. Doi: 10. 1108/02621710610570137.

126 Barrero, Bloom & Davis, 2020.

127 World Health Organization. 2020. *Mental health and psychosocial considerations during the COVID-19 outbreak.* Available from: https://www.who.int/docs/default-source/coronaviruse/mental-health-considerations.pdf

128 Kar S.K., Yasir Arafat S.M., Kabir R., Sharma P. & Saxena S.K. 2020. Coping with Mental Health Challenges During COVID-19. In Saxena S. (ed). Coronavirus Disease. 2019. (COVID-19). *Medical Virology: From Pathogenesis to Disease Control.* Singapore: Springer. https://doi.org/10.1007/978-981-15-4814-7_16

129 Van Hoof. 2020.

130 Takieddine & Al Tabbah. 2020.

131 Gilmore, T.N. & Hirschhorn, L. 1984. Managing human resources in a declining context. In Fombrun, C.J., Tichy, N.M. & Devanna, M.A. (eds). *Strategic Human Resource Management.* New York: John Wiley & Sons, pp. 297-318.

132 Herriot, P. 2001. *The Employment Relationship: A Psychological Perspective.* London: Routledge.

133 Torales, J., O'Higgins, M., Castaldeili-Maia, J.M. & Ventriglo, A. 2020. The outbreak of COVID-19 coronavirus and its impact on global mental health. *International Journal of Social Psychiatry, 66*(4): 317-320.

134 Herriot. 2001. p. 309.

135 Hacker, S. 2010. Zombies in the Workplace. *The Journal for Quality & Participation, 32*(4): 25-28.

136 Turner, D.P. 2020. Sampling Methods in Research Design. *Headache The Journal of Head and Face Pain, 60*(1): 8-12.

137 Bailey, C., Lips-Wiersma, M., Madden, A., Yeoman, R., Thompson, M. and Chalofsky, N., 2019. The five paradoxes of meaningful work: Introduction to the special issue 'meaningful work: Prospects for the 21st century'. *Journal of Management Studies, 56*(3), pp.481-499.

138 Trevor, J. 2019. *Align: A Leadership Blueprint for Aligning Enterprise Purpose, Strategy and Organization: A Leadership Blueprint for Aligning Enterprise Purpose, Strategy and Organisation.* London: Bloomsbury Business, p. 163.

139 Trevor. 2020.

140 Wilson, H.J. & Daugherty, P.R., 2018. Collaborative intelligence: Humans and AI are joining forces. *Harvard Business Review, 96*(4), pp.114-123.

141 Gilmore, T.N. & Hirschhorn, L. 1984. Managing human resources in a declining context. In Fombrun, C.J., Tichy, N.M. & Devanna, M.A. (eds). *Strategic Human Resource Management.* New York: John Wiley & Sons, pp. 297-318.

142 Ibid.

143 Takieddine, H. & Al Tabbah, S. 2020. Coronavirus Pandemic: Coping with the Psychological outcomes, mental changes, and the "new normal" during and after COVID-19. *Open Journal of Depression and Anxiety, 2*: 1-7. Doi: https://doi.org/10.36811/ojda/2020.110005.

144 Mention, A-L., Ferreira, J.J.P. & Torkkeli, M. 2020. Coronavirus: a catalyst for change and innovation. *Journal of Innovation Management 8*(1): 1-5. Doi: https://doi.org/1024840/2183-0606_001-0001.

145 Garg, P. & Rastogi, R. 2006. New model of job design: motivating employees' performance. *Journal of Management Development, 25*(6): 572-587.

146 Zucker, R. 2020. *Managers, adjust your expectations* (without lowering the bar). Harvard Business Review, May: 2-4. Available from: https://hbr.org/2020/05/managers-adjust-your-expectations-without-lowering-the-bar

147 Ibid.

148 Ulrich, D. & Brookbank, W. 2005. *The HR Value Proposition.* Boston, MA: Harvard Business School Press.

149 Garg, P. & Rastogi, R. 2006. New model of job design: motivation employees' performance. *Journal of Management Development, 25*(6): 572-587. Doi: 10. 1108/02621710610570137.

150 Wilson, H.J. and Daugherty, P.R., 2018. Collaborative intelligence: Humans and AI are joining forces. *Harvard Business Review, 96*(4), pp.114-123.

151 Wilson & Daugherty. 2018.

152 Ulrich, D. & Brookbank, W. 2005. *The HR Value Proposition.* Boston, MA: Harvard Business School Press.

153 Trevor, J. 2019. *Align: A Leadership Blueprint for Aligning Enterprise Purpose, Strategy and Organization: A Leadership Blueprint for Aligning Enterprise Purpose, Strategy and Organisation.* London: Bloomsbury Business, p. 161.

154 Trevor. 2019.

INDEX

W